Growing, Growing Strong

A Whole Health Curriculum for Young Children

Connie Jo Smith,
Charlotte M. Hendricks,
and Becky S. Bennett

Redleaf Press
St. Paul, Minnesota

Published by Redleaf Press
a division of Resources for Child Caring
10 Yorkton Court
St. Paul, MN 55117
Visit us online at www.redleafpress.org

©1997 Redleaf Press
Illustrations by Stéphanie Roth

Redleaf Press books are available at a special discount when purchased in
bulk (1,000 or more copies) for special premiums and sales promotions. For
details, contact the sales manager at 800-423-8309.

Library of Congress Cataloging-in-Publication Data
Smith, Connie Jo.
    Growing, growing strong : a whole health curriculum for young
children / Connie Jo Smith, Charlotte M. Hendricks, and Becky S.
Bennett.
        p.   cm.
    Includes bibliographical references (p.).
    ISBN 1-884834-36-1 (alk. paper)
    1. Health education (Preschool)—United States. 2. Health
education (Elementary)—United States. 3. Curriculum planning—
United States. I. Hendricks, Charlotte Mitchell, 1957–   .
II. Bennett, Becky S., 1954–   . III. Title.
LB1140.5.H4S65   1997
372.3'704--dc21   97-26299
                                                            CIP

Manufactured in the United States of America

To my mother Nevolyn, whose healthy genes I hope I inherited.

—CJS

To my son Kevin, who reminds me daily of how much children need to know and how well they can learn.

—CMH

To Judy Whitten, for her dedication and contribution to direct service for young children and her ability to teach us about the importance of health, happiness, and personal growth.

—CJS & BSB

Table of Contents

Introduction

Why Integrate Health Education Into the Early Childhood Curriculum?

This book is created to support the busy teacher who wants to incorporate exciting ideas into the classroom that make health education fun. Whether you and the children are examining a dog's teeth to learn what dentists do or designing clothing for different events and seasons, lots of learning and laughs are guaranteed.

Learning to live a healthy lifestyle begins during the early years of life. For many children, the need for health and safety education becomes a significant reality much too early. Each day approximately 37 children die from accidents, and 685 children are arrested for alcohol or drug offenses. Most accidents and many of the unhealthy lifestyle choices involving children can be prevented when safe and healthy habits are integrated into the classroom curriculum in a nonthreatening, natural way. Infusing the curriculum with health-related information addresses the total day-to-day needs of each child and helps the children practice habits that may well save their lives.

Growing, Growing Strong introduces health information through interactive activities. It allows teachers to customize their approach to meet their classroom goals and the children's goals. The activities, supplemental background information, and resources provide a generous variety of helpful concepts. Pick topics you would like to investigate with children and choose the approach that's right for your classroom. Encourage children's curiosity about themselves, others, and the world around them. Be a "health hit" with *Growing, Growing Strong*.

How This Book Is Organized

Concise information and practical ideas are presented for eight health-related themes. Although the primary focus is health, all subject areas are integrated. Theme concepts overlap and are reinforced throughout the book. Each theme includes sections on diversity, ideas to extend the theme, suggested learning center materials, and recommended activities. Topics in each theme include learning objectives, staff information, environment suggestions, evaluation, a family information and activity bulletin, and child activities. Each theme and each topic can be used independently. Teachers are urged to use the ideas in whatever order meets their needs and the needs of the children. A list of resources to enhance health education for children and adults is provided in the appendix. The resources can be used by staff to enhance their own knowledge, or it can be used to provide information to parents and other teaching team members. In addition to adult resources, child activity books and selected health videos for children are noted and can be used to supplement classroom experiences. The address, telephone number and Internet address is included for a variety of national health-related agencies and associations, many of which have valuable resources available.

Chapters

Each chapter begins with an introduction to the theme and provides general information about why it is important to young children. Characteristics of young children that relate to the theme are reviewed briefly and basic concepts are suggested. Following this general introduction to the theme are a variety of sections, described below, that inspire, support, and reinforce healthy habits in young children,

Addressing Diversity

Emphasizing diversity and inclusion within each theme helps teachers represent all children in the class and encourages respect for differences. This section identifies important considerations for planning activities that all children relate to in some way. Incorporated within the listed activities are materials that represent different races, cultures, physical abilities, communities, and home environments. Celebrating differences also encourages children to learn from one another. Seeking family input and involvement are powerful ways to provide diverse opportunities for children. Throughout this book, teachers are urged to utilize families as resources for adapting and expanding activities. This will ensure accurate representation and inclusion of each family and culture.

Where Will the Theme Lead?

Each theme could lead the class in many different directions, depending upon interests and resources. For each theme, a few words are provided to stimulate ideas for follow-up. Like great cooks, creative teachers may begin with a basic recipe, but often add their own secret "spices." The possibilities with each theme are never-ending once teachers "stir in their own spices." Beginning with a list of words associated to the theme and adding to it expands the possibilities for learning. Observing and listening to children can also guide the expansion of each theme. By individualizing the theme, teachers provide what is perhaps the most beneficial experience—opportunities for children to pursue their related interests.

Knowing the families' interests and priorities for their children can influence how to build upon the themes. Each community offers a wealth of resources that can be used to extend the experiences. Tap into the people and businesses of the community to serve as resources. Remember, too, that the natural environment is a resource that can be studied. Use the listed words as a starting point for ideas.

Learning Center Materials

Learning centers are excellent ways to provide stimulating and developmentally appropriate materials for children to use. A wide range of materials made available in an attractive and organized way enhances learning. Each theme includes a list of supplemental materials suggested for inclusion in the dramatic play, language arts, table toys, science, art, block, and outside learning centers. Pick from the included list or use your own ideas. Add items that are familiar to children and represent their communities. Add a few unfamiliar materials to expose them to new ideas and experiences.

Topics

Each topic begins with brief but specific background information and guidance. Health and safety considerations regarding the lesson are identified and resources suggested. Methods for approaching the topic are incorporated, as are concepts to address within the topic. In some instances, recommended policies are noted.

Learning Objectives

The learning objectives represent health and related concepts and skills that are appropriate for young children. Some children are exposed to health concepts and behaviors as they observe the adults in their homes. As a result, they may come to school already demonstrating the expected levels of awareness and utilization. Children will make progress toward each learning objective at their own rate, and it is appropriate that expectations for meeting the learning objectives will vary. Supplemental objectives based on individual needs may be developed.

Creating the Environment

This section includes ideas for using surrounding environments, such as the classroom and the playground, to reinforce the topic. The teacher's role in preparing and maintaining the environment is discussed. Specific ideas for materials and equipment are also included.

Evaluation

Learning objectives and evaluation go hand-in-hand. The most appropriate assessment involves observing the child to determine mastery of the specific knowledge or skill. Each topic includes questions to guide observation and interaction for assessment purposes. If a child is found to be lacking in health skills, it is usually possible to move the child to an appropriate skill level in a relatively short period of time. Using developmentally appropriate, hands-on learning activities, modeling healthy behavior, and encouraging parents to be actively involved in their child's learning will help the child reach an appropriate skill level.

Family Information and Activity Bulletin

Family involvement is an important component in early childhood health education. Most of what a child learns has its beginnings in the home. Including parents provides continuity between home and school and enhances children's learning in both environments. A "Family Information and Activity Bulletin" is provided for each topic and is intended to extend health education into the home. It can be sent home, incorporated into a newsletter, or posted. Each information sheet provides concise information for families that applies to their child's developmental or health needs. Included in the bulletin is an invitation to provide curriculum ideas and resources, a request for donations of discarded or old materials, and family activities that reinforce the concepts.

Children's Activities

All activities are practical and easy to use. Most can be used in any order. Each topic includes five creative activities and a list of materials needed for implementation. Safety notes are provided for the activities when it would be helpful for staff to identify potential health or safety issues. Most activities also include other suggested ideas related to the topic. The additional activities extend learning and reinforce concepts. They can be implemented with individual children, small groups, or the entire class. Suggested field trips, music, and children's books are included. Teachers are encouraged to modify activities to better meet the interests and needs of the children.

Chapter 1

My Wonderful Body

Every child grows and develops at a different rate. Children vary in height, weight, and motor development. During the preschool years, body proportion changes and children begin to develop a greater sense of balance and more control of large muscle movements, such as running, jumping, and climbing. Fine-motor development also develops more fully during early years as children begin to throw and catch balls, hold crayons, and manipulate small objects.

This theme will help children realize that their bodies are special and work in wonderful ways. Children are naturally curious about their bodies and want to know how body parts work, both separately and together. The activities and resources presented in this theme will help children become aware of their bodies. Children will learn about different body parts and how they work together, differences in body shape and size, and how to take care of their bodies. This knowledge will help children be proud of their bodies.

Addressing Diversity

Incorporate diversity through your choice of words, actions, and materials as well as by inviting diverse people to visit the classroom. A focus on the body is an excellent way to help children begin to examine likenesses and differences and to teach them about acceptance. Talk openly about the body and provide the children with accurate information when they have questions about gender, physical abilities, and skin color.

Ensure that your classroom includes appropriate materials for the varying stages of growth and abilities of children, and that all areas and materials are accessible and safe. Pictures, books, and dolls should reflect different races and cultures, people of different sizes, and people with different physical abilities.

Where Will the Theme Lead?

Use these words to stimulate ideas for follow-up activities:

body parts	itch	strength	hearing aid	jump
shoulders	sunburn	shape	glasses	dance
wrists	muscles	ability	sounds	stretch
belly button	skinny	braille	smell	catch
sweat	big	color of eyes	exercise	roll

Learning Center Materials

Dramatic Play:
dolls with different body types
dolls representing different races
adaptive equipment for dolls
sunglasses and sun hats
knee pads, wrist pads, helmets
eyeglass frames and eye patch
eye chart
herbs and spices
different sizes and textures of fabric

Table Toys:
dollhouse and multiethnic dolls
puzzles representing different races
knob puzzles
paper dolls with protective clothing
lotto games that include body parts
pattern games and cards
eye, ear, nose, mouth, and hand puzzles
matching tactile puzzles and games
grab bag with textured objects

Language Arts:
exercise equipment ads
different kinds of stuffed animals
computer programs that show the body
tape player with headphones
many kinds of music
taped stories/songs about the senses
taped stories/songs about the body
exercise and sports videos
rain stick

Science:
dolls that can be taken apart
charts and posters of the body
x-rays of the body
tape measure
scales
skeleton models and illustrations
sanitized bones (chicken, turkey)
kaleidoscope
see-through music box
stereo speakers to take apart

Blocks:

goggles, helmet
hard hat
work gloves
wooden animals
wooden people of different races
wooden people with different physical abilities
tape measure
work boots
vehicles and ramps

Art:
skull and skeleton artwork
many kinds and colors of paper
   (tracing, tissue, aluminum foil, cellophane,
   gummed, origami, finger paint, metallic,
   carbon, typing, drawing)
many colors of glue
skin-tone colors of paint, crayons, markers,
   pencils, and modeling clay
string, sand, food coloring, cloth, ribbon
supplies for visual and cultural variety

Outdoors:
helmets
work gloves
hard hats
binoculars
periscope
telescope
musical instruments
many sizes of balls
beanbags
riding vehicles

Library Books:
Bein' With You This Way, by
   W. Nikola-Lisa (New York:
   Lee & Low, 1994).
Pretend You're a Cat, by Jean Marzollo and
   Jerry Pinkney (New York: Dial, 1990).
*Cock-A-Doodle-Doo! What Does It Sound Like
   To You?* by Marc Robinson (New York:
   Stewart, Tabori and Chang, 1993).

Topic 1
My Body Parts

Learning Objectives:

☑ Children will identify body parts by correct names.

☑ Children will identify and accept differences in individual appearances.

☑ Children will state or show how to take care of their bodies.

☑ Children will practice behavior that protects specific body parts.

Young children have a natural curiosity about their bodies, especially external body parts that are visible. By learning about and being able to recognize body parts, children can more easily alert adults if they are hurt or injured. Young children may think pain is normal and may not cry when they are seriously injured. For example, when children say "I don't feel good" it is helpful to know if it is their head, stomach, or extremities that hurt. Learning about body parts will enable the child to communicate specific information about what hurts. Also, children may not show signs of an injury, such as a sprained ankle. Watch for changes in behavior or actions, and encourage children to tell an adult when they are hurting.

Identification of body parts also helps children understand and accept differences. Children can recognize such differences as physical ability, height, weight, and color of skin or hair. While young children can see physical differences, they may need help *understanding* how they are alike and different.

Injury prevention and protection of one's body is another component of this topic. Unintentional injury is the leading cause of death for children. Burns, bicycle crashes, and falls from playground equipment or down stairs can cause serious injury or death. Injuries to eyes or ears can cause permanent damage. Help young children learn how to exercise and nurture their bodies, yet protect themselves.

Creating the Environment

Making child-sized helmets available and accessible to children every time they use a wheeled toy helps them practice safe habits. Knee and elbow pads may also be useful protection when children go ice skating, in-line skating, or use riding toys. Gloves are great for picking up trash or digging in the sand. Safety goggles offer protection during woodworking activities. Include materials that are suitable for children at varying stages of physical development and accessible to children with physical disabilities. This may mean providing wheelchair ramps, handrails, and modifying rest rooms and playground equipment.

Evaluation:

☒ Do children use correct names for body parts?

☒ Are children comparing their bodies to others?

☒ Do children use protective clothing in play?

☒ Are children using their bodies in many ways?

☒ Do children use language and actions to show acceptance of their bodies and others?

Family Information & Activity Bulletin

My Body Parts

Young children are curious about their bodies and enjoy naming and counting their body parts. Games are a fun way to help children learn the correct names of body parts.

When your child doesn't feel well, find out which body part hurts. Help your child use correct terms for body parts, rather than nicknames.

Teach your child how to protect body parts. Helmets help prevent head and facial injuries and are worn while bicycling, skating, or skateboarding. Elbow, knee, and wrist pads can prevent serious joint and bone injuries. Many organized sports also require protective gear.

Remember, modeling safe behavior is one of the best ways to teach young children!

Family Activity

☒ Use a tape measure, scales, or other measuring instrument to see how tall each family member is, how long their feet are, and how much they weigh. Show your child the protective gear used by family members, such as sunglasses or goggles, ear plugs, helmets, hard hats, boots, knee pads, and gloves.

Ideas Please

☒ Share with us your ideas for field trips and guest speakers that would help your child learn about body parts and how bodies are alike and different.

Items Please

☒ Send the class old socks and stockings.

Children's Activities

What Is a Body?

Meet with children in small groups and discuss what they know about bodies. Ask questions such as "What is your body made of?" "What are the names of your body parts?" "How is your body like other people's bodies?" and "How is your body different?" Write down what the children say. Explain that they are going to learn more about the body. Ask what they would like to know or what they would like to learn. Use what the children say to help with follow-up.

Materials

large piece of newsprint or poster board, markers

Other Ideas

- Encourage conversation about bodies.

- Visit a museum to see skeletons and bones.

- Help children use their body to make sounds (clapping, snapping, humming, flapping).

- Play the song "Kye Kye Kule," by Tickle Tune Typhoon (*Hug The Earth*, Tickle Tune Typhoon Records).

Body Tour

Arrange a trip to see different representations of bodies. Children can suggest places for the trip. Prepare the children to look at different ways bodies are represented. Ask questions to encourage observation and discussion. Let children sketch what they see.

Places to Visit: art shop or museum with sculptures, photographs, drawings, and paintings; art class with work in progress; lawn and garden store with statues, water fountains, and plaques; clothing stores with mannequins; doll stores; gift stores with figurines; dance studios or recitals.

Materials

paper, pencil

Other Ideas

- Ask children how a stuffed animal's body parts are like their own body parts.

- Visit places to see animal bodies: zoo, humane society, pet stores.

- Read *People*, by Peter Spier (New York: Doubleday, 1980).

- Visit a car garage or body shop and talk about the different car bodies and parts.

Making Bodies

If you went on the field trip (see previous activity), invite children to discuss the different representations of bodies that they saw. Tell them that they can make a body. Encourage them to decide what kind they want to make. They can choose to make a body alone or with the help of their friends. Help them identify the materials they need and make a plan. Facilitate and support as needed. Talk with them about the importance of the skin that will cover the body they make.

Materials

materials identified by children

Other Ideas

- Invite a medical professional to visit the classroom and bring charts, x-rays, and models.
- Invite a veterinarian to visit the classroom and bring animal pictures, charts, and x-rays.
- Read *Your Bellybutton*, by Jun Nanao (Brooklyn, NY: Kane/Miller, 1995).
- Play the song "Skin," by Angie Bolton and Dennis Westphall (*Hug The Earth*. Tickle Tune Typhoon Records).

Protection

Tell children that skin protects the inside part of their bodies by helping to keep germs out and holding our bodies together. Explain that sometimes skin needs protecting too. Show items used to protect the body. Invite them to tell what they know about the items. Ask additional questions like "Who might wear this?" and "Why might someone wear this?" Explain that we need to protect our bodies from harm. Add materials to learning centers for follow-up role-playing.

Materials

goggles, sunglasses, helmets, mouth guard, steel-toe shoes, sunscreen

Other Ideas

- Visit a work place where employees wear protective equipment or clothing.
- Visit a store that sells protective materials.

Body Buddies

Meet with children in small groups and explain that they are to come up with a way to show the other children in the class what they have learned about bodies. They can create and sing a song, make a book and show it, draw a picture and tell about it, present a puppet show, act something out, or use any other ideas they have. Assure them you will provide materials and help them. Support each group and arrange a time for each to share their experiences. Videotape the activities so children can watch themselves, and make the tape available to their families.

Materials

materials identified by children, video camera and tape, VCR and monitor

Other Ideas

- Let children use a computer to write and illustrate a book about what they have learned.

- Invite another class to see the creations.

Topic 2
My Five Senses

Learning Objectives:

☑ Children will identify body parts associated with each of the five senses.

☑ Children will state or show ways to protect their sight and hearing.

☑ Children will identify ways they use their senses.

☑ Children will practice behavior that protects their sight and hearing.

☑ Children will understand and accept that some people may not have full use of all senses.

Children learn by using their senses. Some children may not have full use of all senses or may not have developed an awareness of their senses. Others may rely heavily on certain senses while ignoring other senses. Sensitivity may also change due to illness or external conditions. For example, when one has a cold, the senses of hearing, smell, and taste may change.

We use our senses daily. We use vision, smell, and taste when we eat. We use vision and hearing when crossing a street. And we use touch and vision when working a puzzle. It is important to provide activities and opportunities that encourage the use of and learning through many different senses. In this manner, children with different sensitivities and abilities can participate and contribute to the classroom experience.

Teachers can help children understand the use and importance of the five senses and how to protect the parts of their bodies connected to the senses. Hearing can be protected by limiting the volume of music, especially when in a closed area (such as a car) or when using headphones. Vision can be protected by using goggles and sunglasses, when appropriate, and by avoiding looking at the sun.

Creating the Environment

The classroom and playground may have a variety of objects to explore using the five senses, such as texture boards, scratch and sniff samples, musical instruments, various surfaces, live plants or trees, or other inanimate objects. Protective gear should be accessible to children, such as safety goggles and sunglasses to protect eyes. Make headphones accessible to children to encourage listening.

Evaluation:

☒ Are children discussing their body parts associated with senses?

☒ Do children show curiosity and interest in using their senses?

☒ Are children protecting their hearing by adjusting volume controls appropriately?

☒ Do children protect their sight by wearing goggles or glasses in appropriate situations?

☒ Are children showing sensitivity to people with limited use of senses?

Family Information & Activity Bulletin

My Five Senses

Our five senses—taste, sight, hearing, smell, and touch—are used in everything we do. One way to teach children how senses work together is by cooking a favorite food. Ask your child such questions as "Do you smell the cookies?" "Let's see if they're done," "They look good; should we touch one?" and "They feel warm; should we taste one?" Another example is to teach your child to "stop, look, and listen" before crossing streets. The senses are also used in teaching fire safety. You might tell your children, "If there is a fire, you will hear the smoke alarm, and you may smell the smoke. Feel the door for heat before you open it."

Talk with your child about protecting sight and hearing. Children receive eye injuries while playing with BB guns, sticks, or sharp objects. Talk about how goggles and sunglasses help protect eyes. Protect hearing by keeping the volume low. Loud music can damage hearing.

Family Activities

- Help your child think of as many different ways as possible that people use their senses. Make a list and keep adding to it each day until you run out of ideas.
- Play a game of hide-and-seek that uses visual or auditory clues.

Ideas Please

- Give us ideas for classroom materials to help children learn about their senses.

Items Please

- We would like any extra containers of spices you might have.
- We need to borrow artwork and fabrics of all kinds. They will be displayed and returned.
- We need to borrow music that is special to your family. It will be used carefully and returned.

Children's Activities

Animal Kingdom

Give each child a stuffed animal and ask them to show you the animal's eyes, ears, nose, paws, and mouth. Engage them in a discussion about how the animals might use these parts of their bodies. Then ask children to describe or discuss how they use their own eyes, ears, nose, mouth, feet, and hands. Keep notes about what children have learned and what additional information might be needed or desired.

Safety Note: Check all stuffed animals to ensure that there are no loose parts that children could dislodge, insert in their mouths, and choke on.

Materials
stuffed animals

Other Ideas

- Give each child a doll and have them identify body parts associated with the senses.

- Provide animal puppets and let children demonstrate how each animal uses its senses.

- Provide pictures of animals and let children talk about the body parts used by the senses.

- Play several songs and encourage children to select one that a stuffed animal might like best.

Art Appreciation

Collect diverse pieces of art that look and feel different. Place the art throughout the room, in the hall, and in bathrooms. Art can include mounted pictures from magazines, posters from museums, figurines from garage sales, collages, mobiles made by past classes, calendar pictures and postcards that are reproductions of famous artwork, and greeting cards. Beside each piece of artwork, put an envelope with the artist and the name of the work listed on the front. If the artist isn't credited on the reproduction, write "Unknown" for the artist's name. If work is not named, write "Untitled," or let the children choose a name.

Discuss the characteristics of the art with children and ask questions about how it looks and feels. Tell children about each artist. Ask children to vote for their favorite piece of artwork by placing their name in the appropriate envelope. Assist children as needed with writing their names. Let children help count the names in envelopes to see which artwork received the most votes.

Materials

paintings and drawings, photographs, cards, posters, statues, sculptures, figurines, mobiles, wood carvings, stained glass, wall hangings, rugs, quilts, beadwork, books of artwork, jewelry, paper, pencils, envelopes

Other Ideas

- Provide tools to enhance sight (binoculars, magnifier, microscope, and telescope).

- Visit or invite an optician to the classroom.

- Read *Brown Bear, Brown Bear, What Do You See?* by Bill Martin, Jr. and Eric Carle (New York: Holt, 1983).

A Little Louder Now

Invite the children to dance while you play "Shout" by the Isley Brothers. After the song, tell children in a loud but pleasant voice that some sounds are loud. Slowly lower your voice and say that some sounds are soft. See if children can name loud and soft sounds. Tell children to watch and listen as you clap your hands. Sit and clap very softly. Partially stand up and clap a little louder. Then stand up all the way and clap very loud. Invite children to clap with you. Next, teach the children to watch your hand and to clap softly when it is low, and louder as it gets higher. Try moving from very soft to very loud both gradually and quickly. As follow-up, use this technique for singing, chanting rhymes, stomping, and playing instruments.

Materials

tape or CD player, recording of "Shout" by the Isley Brothers (*The Isley Brothers Story*, Vol. 1, Rhino Records)

Other Ideas

- Visit a music or audio equipment store and listen to music.

- Attend a concert or invite a musician to perform for the class.

- Invite a guest to teach the children sign language.

- Invite a guest to share some words in another language with the children.

- Visit a store that sells hearing aids.

- Visit or invite an audiologist to the classroom.

- Visit an eye, ear, nose, and throat doctor.

Bread Baking

Let children assist in preparing bread to bake. After they have washed their hands, let them examine the breadmaker. Show them the recipe and involve them in measuring and mixing. Ask them questions like, "How much bread do you think this will make?" and "How do you think the breadmaker works?" Show them the timer and set it so that the bread will be finished about the time they will arrive the next day. As they enter, discuss the smell, and after a taste test, discuss the taste. Make additional loaves so they can feel the ingredients, hear the sounds, see the sights, and smell the bread baking, as well as taste it.

Materials

breadmaker, measuring cup, measuring spoons, recipe card, ingredients, knife, serving plates, napkins, various breads to compare

Other Ideas

- Provide foods that taste sour, sweet, salty, and bitter.
- Visit flower shops and smell flowers.
- Visit a bakery and enjoy the smells and tastes.
- To let children learn about the inside of their noses, read *The Holes In Your Nose,* by Genichiro Yagyu (New York: Kane/Miller, 1994).
- Visit an herb garden to taste and smell a variety of herbs.

Satin Sheets

Provide an air mattress and several sheets made from a variety of materials. Large pieces of cloth can also be used as sheets for the mattress. Change the sheets every day and encourage children to feel the "sheet of the day" with a lot of their body parts. Flat sheets could be used without a mattress.

Materials

air mattress, satin sheets, flannel sheets, cotton sheets, netting, burlap, fur

Other Ideas

- Fill containers with objects, materials, and liquids that provide stimulating tactile experiences. Allow children to explore the containers and contents.
- Fill a large box with strips of fabric and encourage children to get into the box and feel them.
- Let children use their feet to feel water, suds, and shaving cream in a washtub.

Topic 3
Moving My Body

Learning Objectives:

☑ Children will understand and show acceptance of different physical abilities.

☑ Children will state or show how exercise helps their body.

☑ Children will participate in physical development activities at levels appropriate to their individual abilities.

Many children love to run, jump, and climb and, if encouraged, will naturally get plenty of exercise. Some children, however, may need more encouragement and assistance in order to participate in movement activities.

Physical development and motor coordination is facilitated by supporting children when they run, jump, balance, throw balls, dance to music, and participate in other noncompetitive movement activities. Encourage children to try a variety of activities, even though the extent to which each child can participate will vary. Promote movement and activity, not competitiveness.

Physical fitness can easily be achieved without expensive equipment or a highly structured exercise program. Large open areas provide the opportunity for running, jumping, and rolling. Parachute activities promote coordination and cooperation. Walking on a simple wooden board placed on the ground promotes balance and coordination. Nature walks are also a fun way to get exercise while integrating discovery and science activities.

When encouraging exercise and movement activities, safety is a consideration. Supervision, education, and the environment are key considerations for child safety. Being aware of children's abilities and encouraging or redirecting activities helps children be successful and safe in a supervised environment. Water play is a favorite of children but requires close supervision since a child can drown in a few inches of water. Safety education can be incorporated daily as children are guided to use equipment appropriately. Children can be provided with the opportunity to develop muscles and gross-motor skills while integrating social skills and safety. Providing a safe environment is an ongoing challenge, but it begins with appropriate equipment and surfaces in a protected area. Toys with wheels should have a wide wheelbase and low center of gravity to provide the most stability. Wading pools or areas with sprinklers should have a nonslip surface, and pool drains must have secure covers to prevent powerful and dangerous suction.

Creating the Environment

An open area large enough for each child to have freedom of movement is helpful for developing physical fitness indoors. The area should be obstacle-free to prevent tripping. The ideal outdoor environment would include age-appropriate playground equipment that meets Consumer Product Safety Commission guidelines. A resilient surface under and around equipment is as important as the equipment itself. Tricycle paths and grassy areas for running and playing contribute to the outdoor environment. A fence or other barrier enhances supervision and safety. An environment free of unsafe equipment, debris, and other potential hazards promotes physical development in a safe manner.

Evaluation:

☒ Are children participating in physical activities?

☒ Is large-motor coordination improving?

☒ Do children discuss exercise, sports, and dance?

☒ Do children show acceptance of their own physical abilities and those of others?

Family Information & Activity Bulletin

Moving My Body

Children need lots of exercise, such as running, jumping, crawling, and climbing. Exercise helps them develop strong muscles and bones, helps their bodies stay healthy and fight off germs that cause sickness, and lets children release energy and relieve stress. Children feel better when they exercise! Be sure your child's play area is safe, both at home and away. Remember, always watch your child when he or she is playing outdoors. Even better, play with your child! Here are some fun activities:

- Help your child think of the different ways that people move their bodies.
- As a family, plan time to be physically active every day for a week. Try different activities.
- Help your child see that there are many different levels of physical ability.

Family Activities

- ☒ Run and jump through sprinklers and water hoses on hot days.
- ☒ Run, jump, and play tag to develop leg muscles.
- ☒ Roll down grassy hills or across the lawn.

Ideas Please

- ☒ Share with us your ideas for games and activities that would help your child learn about moving and staying physically fit.

Items Please

- ☒ Send the class any pictures of people exercising.
- ☒ Please contact us if you are willing to show or loan items that help people move, such as a wheelchairs, crutches, skates, or leg braces.

Children's Activities

In Motion

Prepare a ten-minute video of movement. Include children in the class, family members, other children and adults in the program, strangers, and animals. Provide a diverse video with both males and females, different levels of mobility, and various ages and races. Movement ideas include crawling, walking, sliding, running, biking, skiing, hang gliding, skating, Roller Blading, golfing, swimming, weight lifting, dancing, exercising, washing a car, playing ball, yoga, hopping, jumping, rocking, bending, climbing, horseback riding, hiking, climbing stairs, moving in a wheelchair, and walking with a walker.

Show the video to children. Encourage them to talk about who they saw and what kind of movement they noticed. Introduce words to describe the movements. Write the words so children can see them. Explain that moving our bodies helps us grow strong and stay healthy.

Materials
video camera and tape, VCR and monitor, marker, paper

Other Ideas

- Arrange a trip to a gym so children can see people working out.
- Visit a team during a practice session. Interview the players about why they play, what body parts they move during practice, and how they stay fit.
- Visit a gymnastics class.
- Visit a cheerleading squad during practice. Ask cheerleaders what body parts they exercise.

Bouncing

Provide a bouncing experience for children. It can be on an inner tube, playground equipment with springs, an air mattress, an inflatable construction at an amusement park, a large bouncing ball with a handle, or a minitrampoline.

Consult parents and professionals to determine appropriate ways to include children with physical challenges. Ask children how bouncing felt, what body parts they worked, and what they think made them bounce.

Show children objects and have them guess what will bounce. Let them try to bounce the objects. See if children can figure out how to make those that bounce, bounce higher. Help them measure how high things will bounce. Introduce the word *collision* and explain that there is a collision when there is a bounce. As follow-up, look for collisions.

Safety Note: Limit participation to more closely supervise all bouncing activities. Reinforce proper safety by using appropriate safety equipment.

Materials
bouncing equipment, many kinds of balls, roll of tape, paper, beanbag, inflated beach toys, infant toys, plastic bottles, tape measure

Other Ideas

- While outside, let children in small groups create new passing and bouncing games with various balls.
- Visit a circus to see movement, such as the trapeze artist moving back and forth to gain speed.

Around and Around

Show children a spinning top and ask them how they think it works. Let them play with several tops. Ask children to move like the top and describe the sensation. Provide the children with materials to use for making circular motions outside.

Materials
spinning tops, hula hoops, streamers

Other Ideas

- Visit an amusement park to see and feel the movement of the rides.
- Ask the children to make circular motions with their legs, arms, heads, eyes, fingers, wrists, necks, ankles, and hips.
- Have children hold hands and form a circle. Play music, chanting, or singing, and have the children move to their right, then to their left, then to the center and out again.
- Play the song "Bungee Jumpers," by Sharon Shannon (*A Woman's Heart 2*. Dara Records, 063).

Bending

In a small group, provide children with bendable art supplies. Invite them to create and explore the materials. Ask children how the materials are alike. If they do not use the word *bend*, introduce it and ask them to show what parts of their bodies they can bend. Ask questions to help them identify bending parts like neck, elbows, knees, ankles, wrists, fingers, toes, and waist. Encourage them to show you lots of ways to bend each part they name.

Materials

garbage bag ties, pipe cleaners, vinyl-covered wire, yarn, plastic lacing, Wikki Stix

Other Ideas

- Show children a model or pictures of a skeleton and let them find the places that bend.

- Invite a yoga instructor to visit the classroom and provide a demonstration.

- Visit a dance class or invite a dance teacher to give a classroom demonstration.

- Visit or invite a Tae Kwon Do karate instructor or karate class to give a demonstration.

How Many Ways Can You Move?

Meet with the children in a spacious area and ask them to show you how many ways they can move. Encourage them to find additional ways by watching one another and thinking of animals or machines that move. After a few minutes of moving, ask them to move fast, slow, with someone else, using a prop, without using their feet, with their eyes closed, in a circle, and up and down.

Ask children if they would like to invite their families to come and see the many ways they have learned to move. If the children are interested, form committees and involve them in planning the event. Children may work on invitations, location, greeting families, setting up the seating area, choosing music and decorations, and deciding how to tell families what they know about movement. Encourage children to think ahead about ways they can move and props they may want to use during the event. In order to keep the event spontaneous and stress-free, do not spend time practicing staged movements. Encourage the children to think of ways to involve families in the spontaneous movement. Invite local media to attend the "Moving My Body" show.

Materials
materials identified by children

Other Ideas

- Let children predict movement they will see on a walk and then take them for a walk to observe movement.
- Create an obstacle course or maze for children inside the classroom or outdoors.
- Let children create an obstacle course for themselves or other children.
- Visit a warehouse to see things moved by equipment.
- Read *Sophy and Auntie Pearl*, by Jeanne Titherington (New York: Greenwillow, 1995).

Chapter 2

I Take Care of My Body

As young children become aware of different body parts and understand how the parts work individually and together, they begin to develop an appreciation and accept responsibility for their bodies and their health. Though parents, caregivers, and other adults are primarily responsible for children's health and safety, young children can initiate lifelong habits that will greatly affect their quality of life. Child-learned behaviors such as cleanliness and getting enough rest provide defenses against disease and injury.

Positive body care habits are introduced in this chapter. Activities and resources will help children learn ways to feel good about themselves and their bodies, prevent the spread of disease, gain a measure of independence and control in their lives, and develop self-help skills.

Addressing Diversity

Learn about family habits and beliefs regarding bathing, hair care, going to the dentist, clothing styles, and children dressing themselves. Recognize that some cultures do not encourage as much independence in young children as others. As topics are introduced, encourage children to see, feel, and hear similarities and differences, and then to discuss what they observe. Use questions to reinforce discussion and broaden knowledge, which helps children accept other people and their differences.

Intervene if children make fun of others who look different or have different skills. It is appropriate and helpful for children to ask questions and discuss thoughts, but it should be done in a considerate way.

Where Will the Theme Lead?

Use these words to stimulate ideas for follow-up activities:

rest	plumbing	salon	cavity	zipper
wash	comb	toothbrush	sew	pillow
towels	shampoo	floss	tunic	blanket
bathrooms	braid	detergent	fabric	dreams
disease	turban	clothesline	Velcro	routines

Learning Center Materials

Dramatic Play:
doll diapers and changing table
baby bathtub
dolls with hair and teeth
shampoo and creme rinse containers
ribbons, scarves, bows, barrettes
hair dryer (without cords)
empty toothpaste containers
sleepwear and robes
various fabric pieces
dream catchers
clothesline, clothespins

Table Toys:
PVC pipe pieces
water to clean toys
bath toys to sort
belts to fasten
buttons to sort
boots to lace
shoes to tie
shoes with Velcro straps
lacing cards
soap shapes for sorting

Language Arts:
finger and hand puppets
hairstyle magazines that include
 minorities and diverse styles
sewing patterns
clothing catalogs
luggage tags
sleeping bags
pictures of teeth
lava lamp
wave machine
aquarium

Science:
objects that sink and float, bath toys
bathtub fixtures
cuttings from a hairstylist
replicas of teeth teeth, impressions
teeth x-rays that show roots
vegetables rooting in water
dental records
shoes, shoe shine kit
flashlights and flashlight parts
massager

Blocks:
work gloves
carpenter's belt
pictures and props to build hotels
pictures and props to build beds
clothespins
bath toys
hair rollers
washcloths
shampoo bottles
toothpaste and soap cartons
shoe and hat boxes

Art:
finger paints
materials for hand models: clay,
 Styrofoam, papier-mâché supplies,
 short pieces of vinyl-covered wire
wig-making supplies: yarn, string,
 shower cap, swim cap
painter's brushes, vegetable brushes,
 toothbrushes, hairbrushes
fabric scraps
glow-in-the-dark paint, chalk, stickers

Outdoors:
moist disposable towelettes
wading pool
water hose and sprinkler
hammock
sleeping bags
tent
bucket of soapy water and
 sponge to wash trikes
work gloves

Library Books:
Stellaluna, by Janell Cannon
 (San Diego, CA: Harcourt, 1993).
Hats Off to Hair, by Virginia Kroll
 (Watertown, MA: Charlesbridge, 1995).
Shoes, Shoes, Shoes, by Ann Morris
 (New York: Lothrop, 1995).
King Bidgood's In The Bathtub, by Audrey
 Wood (San Diego, CA: Harcourt, 1985).

Topic 1
Washing Myself

Learning Objectives:

☑ Children will know when to wash hands.

☑ Children will practice appropriate hand washing.

☑ Children will state reasons for taking a bath.

Proper hand washing and bathing protect against communicable diseases. Hands come in contact with a multitude of germs. Children's hands pick up contaminated toys, play in dirt or sand, cover coughs and sneezes, and touch the hands of other children. Proper hand washing and bathing removes most harmful germs before they spread to mouths, noses, eyes, or other people. Cleanliness is important to prevent infection of cuts, scratches, irritated skin, and sores. Cleanliness may also promote self-esteem in children.

Most children know they should wash hands before eating and after going to the bathroom. It is also important for them to wash hands before cooking activities, before and after sand and water play, after coughing or sneezing (even if they used a tissue), after playing with animals, after playing outdoors, or anytime their hands appear dirty.

Because running water rinses away germs, it is best for washing hands and bathing. Bacteria can live and multiply on bar soap; therefore liquid soap, particularly antibacterial soap, is recommended. Children should thoroughly dry off after washing. Remaining moisture not only provides a place for germs to live, but can also lead to chapped or irritated skin.

A child's skin is much more tender than an adult's. Even a brief exposure to hot water can cause second and third degree burns. Teachers can encourage children to learn to turn on and carefully regulate water temperature.

Adult modeling promotes proper hand washing. Teachers should wash their hands at the times described above, after assisting children with going to the bathroom or blowing noses, and after picking up toys or putting away food and dirty dishes. After diapering a child, teachers should wash hands and assist the child in washing her/his hands. Train and monitor classroom volunteers to assure that they practice appropriate hand washing procedures.

It is equally important that teachers wear disposable latex gloves when assisting children in the bathroom, diapering, cleaning up blood or body fluids, and picking up and disposing of trash. Gloves should be worn only once and, after removing, hands should be washed.

Creating the Environment

The ideal environment would include a sink with warm, running water, liquid soap, paper towels, and a wastebasket within children's reach. Hot water temperature should not exceed 120° Fahrenheit. Water temperature can be controlled either by adjusting the hot water heater or by installing a temperature regulator.

Have children create and post signs in the classroom to remind themselves and adults to wash their hands.

Evaluation:

☒ Do children wash hands correctly?

☒ Are children talking about washing their hands and bathing?

☒ During play, are children washing dolls?

Family Information & Activity

Bulletin

Washing Myself

Washing and bathing help prevent the spread of disease, infection of cuts and scratches, and irritated skin and sores. Help your child learn to wash hands before eating or preparing food, after playing outside or with pets, after sneezing or using tissues, and after using the toilet. Liquid soap (especially antibacterial soap) is best. Rinse hands under running water and dry them thoroughly. If soap and water aren't available, premoistened towelettes can be used.

Bathtime provides opportunity for parents to discuss water safety with children. There are many important aspects of water safety. For example, children can easily slip and injure themselves, get severe burns from hot water, or drown in just a few inches of water. A child's skin is much more tender than an adult's. Hot water temperature should be no more than 120° Fahrenheit and can be controlled by adjusting the water heater or by installing a temperature regulator.

Family Activities

☒ Take your child with you when you shop for bathing and hand washing supplies.

☒ Let your child help select items he/she needs to take a bath or shower and clean clothes to wear afterward.

Ideas Please

☒ Share with us ideas for field trips and speakers that would help children learn about hand washing and bathing.

Items Please

☒ Send the class magazines or catalogs with pictures of hands, soaps, and bathroom accessories.

©1997 Redleaf Press, *Growing, Growing Strong*

Children's Activities

Hands of Friends

Encourage children to examine their hands to see unique characteristics. Have them look for differences in palm lines and fingerprint lines. Point out and discuss any moles, freckles, calluses, wrinkles, scars, or other distinguishing marks. Explain that we can show our hands to someone else to examine, but we should not touch someone unless they say it is okay. See if children want to show their hands to a friend. Help children compare the sizes, shapes, and different colors of hands. Tell the children to compare their fingernails to other fingernails to see how they are alike and different. Provide magnifying glasses and measuring instruments.

Materials
magnifying glasses, rulers, tape measures

Other Ideas

- Encourage children to ask family members if they can examine their hands.
- Photograph and display pictures of hands in a variety of positions (palm up, palm down, folded, fist).
- Let children make model hands using materials they identify.
- Visit a medical facility or store that has prosthetic devices.
- Visit a store to see mannequin hands and find out how the hands are used.
- Visit a museum or art store to see pictures and sculptures of hands.
- Photocopy and display images of children's hands.

Hand Washing Interview

Tell children that they will interview people about hand washing. Encourage them to think of questions. List their questions and add to the list as children think of others.

Arrange a time for adults to be interviewed by a small group of children. Select people who wash their hands because of their jobs, such as nurses, doctors, preschool teachers, cooks, food servers, janitors, artists, sanitation workers, dentists, and mechanics. Children could take a field trip to conduct their interview or invite guests to the classroom. Give each small group a chance to report to another group about their interview.

Materials
paper, marker

Other Ideas

- Prepare and show a video of people, including family members, being interviewed about how they take care of their hands.

- Look for posted signs about hand washing.

- Visit a salon and let the children watch how fingernails are manicured.

- Visit a physical therapist to learn about hand exercises.

- Visit a doctor to see pictures and learn about the bones, muscles, tendons, joints, ligaments, and cartilage in hands.

Lather Up

In small groups, show children the correct hand washing procedure and encourage them to practice the following: 1) Run water and adjust temperature appropriately. 2) Wet hands under running water. 3) Apply liquid antibacterial soap and rub hands to create a lather. 4) Rub hands thoroughly to clean the wrists, palms, fingers, in between fingers, the back of hands, and around fingernails. 5) Rinse hands. 6) Dry hands thoroughly using a clean paper towel or air dryer. 7) Dispose used paper towel in wastebasket.

Materials

warm running water, liquid antibacterial soap, clean paper towel or air dryer, trash can

Other Ideas

- Let children dip hands in paint and make handprints. Practice washing hands afterwards.

- Involve children in making reminder signs to wash hands before they eat, after they paint, after they go to the bathroom, after they blow their noses, before and after they play in sand or water, and whenever their hands are dirty.

- While children are washing their hands, ask them where they think the water goes when it goes down the drain. Help them investigate, if there is interest.

- Visit a water treatment plant to see where water goes when it leaves the sink.

- Visit a water tower, well, or other source to see where water comes from.

- Visit rivers, ponds, mud puddles, and lakes.

- Visit a construction site to see a building's plumbing system.

Bathtub and Shower Model

Ask the children to think of ways to make a shower and bathtub that could be used in the classroom for role-playing. Encourage them to think of the materials they need and the steps involved in creating a shower or tub. Ask specific questions to help them create realistic and life-sized models, such as "How will you know what size to make the bathtub?" Keep notes on the children's ideas so you can guide and remind them. Provide the materials requested and the guidance to help children succeed. Place the models they make in an appropriate place to encourage play. Take pictures or videotape children as they work on and play with the model. Put the pictures or video where children and parents can view them.

Materials

measuring tools, large cardboard boxes, old fixtures, pipes, other materials identified by children

Other Ideas

- Visit any bathroom facility in the classroom building or on the grounds.

- Visit stores that sell bathtubs and showers, and examine them.

- Visit a locker room and let children take a shower with their swimsuits on.

- Interview people to see if they prefer baths or showers.

- Create a tape of music or water sounds to listen to while bathing.

- Listen to the song "Crowded Tub" by Gilda Radner (*Free to Be… A Family.* A&M, 5196).

- Read *No More Water In The Tub!* by Tedd Arnold (New York: Dial, 1995).

Baby Bath

Using a baby bathtub and doll, show how to bathe a baby. Talk about the water temperature, soap, lathering each body part, rinsing, and drying. Ask children why it is important to bathe babies. Provide bathing materials and dolls for children to use for role-playing.

Materials

water, soap, washcloths, towels, dolls, baby bathtub

Other Ideas

- Show a variety of bath toys and ask children what they know about them.

- Show children various bath and shower accessories and ask them to explain how the objects are used.

- Encourage children to make a book that they can share with younger children to help them understand how to take a bath.
- Visit a car wash and talk to the workers about why people get their cars washed.
- Visit a dog groomer or veterinarian and observe a dog bath.
- Visit a park or nursery and look for birdbaths.
- Play "Bathtime," by Raffi (*Everything Grows*. Shoreline, 10039).
- Read *Little Elephant*, by Tana Hoban and Miela Ford (New York: Greenwillow, 1994).

Topic 2
I Take Care of My Hair

Learning Objectives:

☑ Children will groom hair on dolls or self.

☑ Children will wash dolls' hair in dramatic play.

☑ Children will state reasons to wash hair.

☑ Children will show acceptance of different hairstyles.

The idea of what constitutes hair grooming varies greatly. It may involve combing or brushing, using a pick, or putting in barrettes and ribbons. Children with very short or almost shaved hair may just need to "brush" over the head with a dry cloth to remove sand or dirt. Teachers must be sensitive to various hair-grooming techniques that are based on the characteristics of hair (straight or curly, oily or dry, texture). Hairstyles may also vary based on personal or cultural differences. Use correct terminology for the classroom population's hairstyles, cuts, hair care procedures, and products.

Clean, well-groomed hair is important for reasons other than appearance. Dry scalp (dandruff) can cause itching, and scratching can cause skin conditions such as eczema or impetigo. Parasites such as head lice can also live in the hair, and it is easier to spot and remove lice and nits (lice eggs) from well-groomed hair. Head lice prefer clean, dry hair with a smooth texture so they can attach their nits to the hair shaft. Lice do not like hair with a coarse texture.

Creating the Environment

Children can be encouraged to groom their hair when it is appropriate. After playing outside, children may want to brush, comb, or shake sand and dirt from their hair. Use individual brushes, combs, and picks that can be stored in each child's individual storage space after use. Mirrors may encourage children to look at and care for their hair.

Evaluation:

☒ Do children talk about hairstyles in accepting ways?

☒ During play are children grooming their hair or a doll's hair?

☒ Are children talking about hair care and involving it in their role-playing?

Family Information & Activity Bulletin

I Take Care of My Hair

Even young children can learn about hair care. Explain how you care for your child's hair. If interested, let your child participate in hair care, including washing hair, combing or picking, adding products or accessories (gel, barrettes, or ribbons), and providing special care (such as getting rid of lice).

Head lice are tiny bugs that live in people's hair. They are usually dark tan, brown, or black, and as small as a dot. Lice eggs attach to hair near the scalp. Head lice spread by head-to-head contact or by sharing such objects as hats, combs, pillows, or headphones.

If your child has lice, the entire family should be checked. Treat only those family members that have lice. Call your child's doctor, the health department, or a pharmacist and ask about special shampoos for head lice. Do not use these shampoos on infants, or if you are pregnant or nursing. Some lice shampoos do not kill the nits (eggs). Nits must be removed by using a special comb.

Because lice can live on clothing, beds, or other personal items, soak all washable items in hot water for 10 minutes or wash in hot water and dry in a hot dryer. Vacuum carpets and furniture.

Family Activities

- [X] Look at family photos and talk about how each member's hair has changed over the years.
- [X] Allow your child to try different hairstyles or ways to groom hair.

Ideas Please

- [X] Give suggestions of hair care products to learn about.

Items Please

- [X] Send the class empty hair care containers and magazines about hairstyles.
- [X] Please give us any broken hair dryers, curling irons, or other hair care appliances.

Children's Activities

Hairstyles

Show the children several dolls, both male and female, with different kinds of hair. Ask them how the dolls are alike and how they are different. If no one mentions the hair, ask specific questions like, "How is this doll's hair different from this one's?" "Which doll's hair is curly?" "Which doll's hair do you like the best?" Help children see differences in color, length, texture, and style of hair.

Materials
dolls with different kinds of hair

Other Ideas

- Encourage children to look in a mirror and study and talk about their own hair.
- Visit a store that sells dolls to see all of the doll hairstyles.
- Visit a wig store and look at the wide selection.

Hair Snapshots

Invite several guests to attend a hairstyle photo shoot and interview session in the classroom. Prepare a diverse guest list that includes males and females, as well as individuals of different races. Plan to have many colors, lengths, textures, and styles of hair represented. Invite a woman with short hair and a man with long hair. Include some family members of the children in the class. As guests are invited, prepare them for the children's questions. Invite a local television or newspaper reporter to cover the event.

Let children practice using a camera without film before the photo shoot. Show them photographs or magazine pictures as samples. Explain that lots of people take pictures, and that professional photographers take pictures as part of their jobs.

During the visit, take more than one picture of each guest for classroom discussion and activities. Photographs can show the front, side, and back views. Place pictures in a photograph album for future reference. Also help children think of questions they may want to ask about the guests' hair, such as "How do you take care of your hair?"

Materials
camera, film, photograph album

Other Ideas

- Give children the opportunity to select and use materials to create a model of hair.
- Videotape a wide variety of commercials that show people with various types and styles of hair.
- Have children observe and describe other hairstyles.

Washing Hair

Ask children to tell all they know about washing hair. Encourage them to share how they feel about getting their hair washed, why people wash their hair, what supplies are needed to wash hair, and the steps in washing hair.

After the discussion, show children the supplies for washing hair and a doll that needs its hair washed. Show children how to wash the hair and keep the soap out of the eyes. Put the doll and hair-washing supplies in the dramatic play center so children can experience washing a doll's hair.

Materials

baby shampoo, clean water, towel, doll with hair

Other Ideas

- Visit a hairstylist or barber to observe the work being done and ask questions.
- Visit a school that trains hairstylists or barbers.

Haircut

Contact a hairstylist to request samples of clean hair cuttings. Show the children the pieces of hair and ask what they think it is. Explain how you got the hair. Let the children examine it under a microscope, under a magnifying glass, and with the naked eye. Put the hair in the science center for children to continue their study.

Materials

hair, microscope, magnifying glass, tweezers, sandwich bags or other containers for hair samples

Other Ideas

- Go for a walk to discover hair on animals and other people.
- Show pictures of you at different ages so children see that hair changes.
- Encourage the children to look at their baby pictures to see that their hair changes.

Take Care

Tell the children that they can each make a poster that tells how to take care of hair. Talk with them before they begin, and help them plan what they want to say or show. Let children select materials to create their posters. Support children by providing materials and assisting with writing, if requested. Listen to children and look at their messages to see what level of understanding they have about hair care. Encourage children to take their posters home and use them to tell their families what they know about taking care of hair.

Materials

poster board, writing utensils, art supplies, magazine pictures, other materials identified by children

Other Ideas

- Take children to visit a store that sells hair products or accessories and buy some for the classroom.
- Make a video or audio recording of children explaining how to care for hair.

Topic 3
Brushing My Teeth

Learning Objectives:

☑ Children will correctly brush teeth.

☑ Children will know when to brush teeth.

☑ Children will state reasons to brush teeth.

☑ Children will state how a dentist helps them take care of their teeth.

The purpose of toothbrushing is to remove food from teeth. When food is not removed, bacteria grows and forms plaque (a film on the teeth). This plaque can lead to decay (cavities). Although it is recommended that children brush every time they eat, this is not always possible. Teachers can encourage toothbrushing and help children develop skills by providing an opportunity for children to brush their teeth each day.

Keep in mind that only a "pea size" amount of toothpaste is recommended, since young children often swallow the toothpaste and saliva. Supervise children while brushing and help them check their teeth after brushing. If brushing is not possible, provide disposable cups and encourage children to "swish and spit" with water to rinse food off teeth.

Young children should not use mouthwash or rinses because they often swallow the fluid, which may contain alcohol, fluoride, or other ingredients. In large amounts, these can be harmful to young children.

Limiting certain kinds of food is helpful in maintaining healthy teeth. Some foods stick to teeth more than others. The sugar in hard or sticky candy stays on teeth longer than the sugar in chocolate bars or birthday cake. Dried, processed fruit snacks sound healthy but may not be good for teeth. Children may eat these foods occasionally, but it is best to have food, including sweets, at meals or designated snack times, rather than throughout the day. Encourage children to brush or rinse teeth immediately after meals and snacks.

Children should visit a dentist at least every six months, or more often if needed. Teachers can discuss with children how dentists and dental hygienists help us take care of our teeth. Care should be taken not to frighten children; rather, discuss points such as how to open the mouth, how the mirror helps the dentist see teeth, and special ways the dentist brushes teeth.

Creating the Environment

For daily toothbrushing, a water source and rinsing receptacle are necessary. Each child should have a child-sized, soft-bristle toothbrush labeled with his or her name, (or use disposable toothbrushes). After use, store upright in a container that allows the toothbrushes to air-dry without touching one another.

Provide each child with individual toothpaste tubes labeled with their names, or distribute toothpaste on wax paper squares for each child. A single tube of toothpaste that touches each child's toothbrush should not be used. Use disposable cups to rinse after brushing, if possible.

Evaluation:

☒ Do children correctly brush their teeth?

☒ Have children asked to brush teeth at appropriate times?

☒ Can children tell why brushing is important?

☒ Do children involve dental care in their play?

☒ Can children tell how a dentist helps care for their teeth?

Family Information & Activity Bulletin

Brushing My Teeth

Teeth are important, even baby teeth! Preschoolers usually have twenty teeth. Permanent teeth start to come in when children are about six years old.

Help your children clean teeth and gums every day. The most important time to brush is before going to bed. Children swallow less during the night, and bacteria has a chance to build up in the mouth if food particles are present.

Children should brush for about five minutes with a small, soft-bristle toothbrush and a "pea-sized" amount of toothpaste. Check your child's teeth and have them brush any spots missed. Mouthwashes and fluoride rinses are not recommended for young children, since they may contain alcohol, fluoride, or other ingredients that can be harmful if swallowed in large amounts.

Family Activities

☒ Help prepare children for a visit to the dentist. Discuss how dentists and hygienists help take care of teeth. Look at each other's teeth in the mirror and discuss how dentists use a small mirror to see teeth. Practice opening your mouths to see who can open the widest. Do not focus on shots, drills, pain, or other scary aspects.

Ideas Please

☒ Give us your ideas for field trips and guest speakers that would help your child learn about taking care of his/her teeth.

Items Please

☒ Send the class empty toothpaste boxes.

Children's Activities

Toothbrush Examination

Hold up a toothbrush and ask children to describe what it is and how it is used. Show the children another toothbrush that's different because of size, color, shape, or type of bristles, and ask if it is a toothbrush too. Display many different kinds of toothbrushes to examine and discuss.

Materials

a variety of unused toothbrushes

Other Ideas

• Visit a store to see different dental-related items.

• Let children experiment by painting with a variety of brushes.

• Play the song "Pearly White Waltz," by Tickle Tune Typhoon (*All of Us Will Shine*. Tickle Tune Typhoon Records).

Toothbrush Wiggle

Have a small group of children wiggle and jiggle their fingers, arms, legs, and whole bodies. Tell the children that when they brush their teeth, they should "wiggle and jiggle" their toothbrush on all parts of their teeth. See if children can show you their upper teeth, lower teeth, biting surfaces, inner surfaces, and outer surfaces. Show children the correct way to brush teeth and let them practice. Label toothbrushes and store them in a way that allows plenty of air to circulate around them but doesn't allow them to touch one another.

Materials

toothbrush for each child, toothpaste, storage container

Other Ideas

- Visit a dentist to see dental equipment and tools, and to sit in the chair.

- Let children use a mirror to examine their own teeth.

- Encourage children to move up, down, and around when music is played. Then show them how to move their toothbrushes up, down, and around.

- Play "Reggae Rock," by Michigan and Smiley (*Reggae for Kids.* RAS 3095).

Sticky Snacks

Gather a variety of sticky things for children to explore. Invite children to touch the different things and talk about how each feels. While children are washing their hands, ask which things are the easiest and which are the hardest to wash off, and why.

Tell the children that some foods are sticky and some are not. See if children can name some foods that are, and are not, sticky. Give the children a snack that consists of something sticky and something that is not sticky. Have them tell which is sticky and how it feels in their mouths. Ask children why sticky food is not good for us to eat. End the activity with everyone brushing their teeth.

Materials

individual toothbrushes, toothpaste, sticky items (contact paper, honey, syrup, raisins, marshmallows, glue, hair gel, stickers), nonsticky items (string, apples, buttons, popcorn, carrots, fabric, nuts, rocks, crackers)

Other Ideas

- Provide pictures of sticky and nonsticky things for children to sort.

- Add sticky things to the art center.

Gum It

Ask children what they think the inside of a baby's mouth looks like and what they think babies eat. Then invite a parent with a baby to visit the classroom. Help children decide what questions to ask the parent about the baby. After the visit, include the children in writing a thank-you note.

Materials

paper, crayons

Other Ideas

- Visit a farm, petting zoo, or pet store to see the teeth of many different animals.

- Visit a park or plant nursery to look for plant roots. Ask the employees to explain to children why the roots are important.

Breanne Brushes

Involve children in creating individual toothbrushing charts. Ask the children to mark their chart when they brush their teeth. Observe to see if they used appropriate technique and if they brushed long enough. After they brush, show them a doll and tell them that the doll's name is Breanne. Tell them she does not want to brush her teeth. Ask them to help Breanne understand why it is important to brush. Listen to their reasons to assess their level of understanding.

Materials

toothbrush, toothpaste, water, heavy paper or construction paper, markers, rulers, doll, individual toothbrushes

Other Ideas

- Tape record children explaining why toothbrushing is important.

- Encourage children to create a poem or song about toothbrushing.

Topic 4
I Dress Myself

Learning Objectives:

☑ Children will participate in dressing activities.

☑ Children will develop fine-motor skills necessary in dressing.

☑ Children will identify clothing appropriate for weather conditions.

☑ Children will identify clothing appropriate for various activities.

☑ Children will see and accept different clothing styles.

Introduce children to how clothing helps us stay healthy. Warm clothing protects us from cold weather or wind, raincoats shield us from rain, lightweight clothing keeps us from getting too warm, and shoes protect our feet and toes. Shoes also help protect feet from glass or other debris, insect stings, and bites.

Clothing can pose dangers as well. If caught on play equipment or stair rails, drawstrings on hoods may strangle young children. Necklaces, rings, and hoop earrings can also catch on equipment and cause injury.

Children have temperature preferences. Some children are comfortable in short sleeves year-round, while others want to wear sweaters. Encourage children to recognize and express when they are uncomfortable (for example, too hot or cold) and to take appropriate action (take off or put on a jacket).

Children have limited control over what clothing is available. Some families may not have appropriate outerwear or appropriate sizes; however, a child without a warm coat at school may simply be stating a preference. If a family is in need of clothing, you may want to check available program or community resources. When offering assistance to families, be sensitive to their feelings.

Be aware that clothing choices may be related to family, cultural, or religious background. Clothing is a significant part of individual and group identification. Learn correct terminology and significance for special clothing used by the families in your classroom and community. As long as children's safety or health is not at risk due to clothing, be accepting of family choices.

Staff may refer to *Children Just Like Me*, by Sue Copsey (New York: Dorling Kindersley, 1995). This book provides pictures and information about clothing from around the world. It is important that educators help avoid stereotyping by learning the differences between clothes worn for celebration and daily living. Ann Morris provides examples of clothing diversity in her book *Hats, Hats, Hats* (New York: Lothrop, 1989). She shows that covering one's head can be for decoration, respect, or worship.

Creating the Environment

Encourage self-help skills, independence, and decision-making by providing each child with an accessible place to hang or store coats, hats, and other clothing. A wide variety of clothes and accessories for dramatic play can give children the opportunity to become familiar with clothing for different activities, celebrations, cultures, and weather.

Evaluation:

- ☒ Do children show a preference for some styles, yet accept people with different preferences?

- ☒ Do children take an active part in dressing themselves after going to the bathroom and when going outside?

- ☒ During play, are children trying on a variety of clothes?

- ☒ Are children talking about clothes for different situations?

Family Information & Activity Bulletin

I Dress Myself

Your child is learning about appropriate dress for health. Let your child wear comfortable play clothes to school. He or she may dig in dirt, roll in the grass, and paint pictures. Clothes need to be washable. Shorts or jeans and pullover shirts may be most comfortable. Although it may be cold outside, your child can get hot while running and playing hard. Layers of clothes can be removed if he or she gets too warm.

Closed shoes with rubber soles, such as sneakers, help to protect the feet. Wearing socks helps prevent blisters.

Open shoes and shoes with slick soles can cause tripping and falling.

Avoid clothes with drawstrings, especially on hoods. They can catch on play equipment and strangle your child. Necklaces, rings, or earrings can also catch on equipment and cause injury.

Family Activities

- ☒ Pick out two outfits that are acceptable and let your child pick which one to wear. Talk about why either outfit would be okay.

- ☒ Encourage children to button, snap, and zip their own clothes. Avoid clothing that children can't easily fasten.

Ideas Please

- ☒ Give us ideas for helping your child learn about clothes and getting dressed.

Items Please

- ☒ Send the class extra buttons, clothes for dress up, accessories, and coat hangers. Please share clothes, buttons, or fabric special to your family for us to display and return.

Children's Activities

Unpacking

Select suitcases of different sizes, shapes, materials, handles, and designs. Pack each with clothes for dolls, children, adults, work, play, dress up, all seasons, and from many cultures.

Talk with the children about how the suitcases are alike and different, and let them move the suitcases around. Let them guess what's inside. Write their guesses on a large piece of paper. Vote to see which suitcase will be opened first.

Involve children in opening and removing clothes one at a time. Ask children to describe the clothes. Talk about where and who might have worn the clothes and in what kind of weather. As each item is discussed, have a child put the garment in a dirty clothes hamper, hang up the item, or fold it for storage. Repeat the steps with a few of the pieces of clothing. Not all suitcases will be unpacked. This activity can be distributed over several days until the suitcases are empty. Leave empty suitcases in a designated place for children to use in role-playing.

Materials

paper, marker, different suitcases, a wide variety of clothes, clothes hangers, several kinds of dirty clothes hampers

Other Ideas

• Let children sort clothes according to the categories rain, sun, or snow.

• Have children sort clothes according to where on the body they might be worn.

Rinse It, Wring It, Hang It

Prior to this activity, select a few pieces of washable clothing and put them in a dirty clothes hamper. Gather a small group of children and have them each get something out of the hamper. Ask where they put dirty clothes at home. Tell them that most clothing has a tag sewn inside, and ask what they think is on the tag. After they locate the tags, read each one to the children. Provide supplies and let children wash a piece of clothing, rinse it, wring it, and hang it on an inside or outside clothesline. Allow children to feel and smell the clothes at different stages.

Materials

washable clothes, dirty clothes hamper, washtub or dish pan, water source, hypoallergenic detergent, fabric softener, stain remover, clothesline, clothespins

Other Ideas

- Invite children to wash doll clothes.
- Tour a dry-cleaning business.
- Visit a coin-operated laundry and use the machines.

Grand Opening

Ask children what they would need to know if they opened a clothing store. Visit a clothing store to learn about the merchandise and the store operation. Help children think of things to ask, and let them look, listen, and sketch during the visit. After the visit, encourage discussion about clothes they saw, music or other sounds they heard, and equipment used by employees. Help children make lists of things to do and things they need to set up a store. Guide the activities and provide needed materials to set up a special clothing store learning center.

Materials

materials identified by children

Other Ideas

- Visit a clothing store that has children's clothes.
- Visit a shoe store or a shoe repair shop.
- Visit a store that sells closet organizers.
- Visit a home with lots of closets.
- Play "Sneakers," by Tickle Tune Typhoon (*Circle Round.* Tickle Tune Typhoon Records).

Developing Designs

Ask children what clothes they like. Explain that someone designed their clothes, and that some people do this as their job. Tell them that one way to design clothes is to draw an idea first. Show them clothing patterns. See if they want to design clothes. Help them think about the steps for creating clothes and provide materials to foster their new designs.

Materials

pencils, tissue paper, glitter, lace, sequins, aluminum foil, bows, ribbons, yarn, netting, scarves, clothespins, scissors, silk flowers, glue, feathers, soft fabric, metallic fabric, sewing patterns, other materials identified by children

Other Ideas

- Visit a sewing factory.
- Invite a tailor or seamstress that makes clothes or performs alterations to come speak to the class.
- Read *Jesse Bear, What Will You Wear?* by Nancy White Carlstrom (New York: Aladdin, 1996).

Fashion Show

Describe a fashion show, and talk about its purpose of letting people see new clothes. Explain to children how people assist with producing a fashion show in different ways. Discuss the following steps in planning and presenting a fashion show: 1) selecting clothes, 2) writing a description of the clothes to announce during the show, 3) deciding where and when it will be, 4) getting lights for the show, 5) selecting music to play, 6) advertising the show, 7) deciding who will operate lights, who will play music, and who will be models in the show.

Ask children if they would like to plan and have a fashion show. If there is interest, have children volunteer for committees and begin small-group work. Videotape the show for children to watch and talk about. Invite the news media to the show or send pictures and a report.

Materials

clothes to model, stage decorations, instruments or taped music, lights for the stage, paper, pencils, blank tape, video camera, VCR, monitor

Other Ideas

- Visit a fashion show or a rehearsal for a fashion show.
- Let children have a doll fashion show.
- Visit a mall and have children look at the many different clothing styles people are wearing.

Topic 5

I Need My Rest

Learning Objectives:

☑ Children will express feelings about rest time and nighttime.

☑ Children will state reasons we need rest.

☑ Children will practice relaxation activities.

☑ Children will experience fun activities in the dark.

Many young children need rest or relaxation at some time during the day. Children may become exhausted, overstimulated, or stressed without being aware of how they are feeling. Physical exhaustion and overstimulation increase stress and the resulting changes in energy levels are often misjudged and treated as misbehavior. Helping children learn to recognize when they are tired or stressed and how to rest or relax may help reduce inappropriate behaviors and, in some cases, physical illness.

Programs may schedule a rest period, or they may encourage children to rest whenever they need it. Some children go to sleep easily, while others may only rest. Some might be unable to rest quietly if they already have adequate rest, if they are just too excited about other activities, or if they fear the dark, being alone, or being abused.

When preparing for rest time, encourage children to help with cot placement and to get their sheets and/or blankets from individual storage spaces. Provide relaxation activities and a soothing environment leading into and during rest time. If a child cannot rest, provide alternative relaxing and quiet activities, such as looking at books or coloring.

To assure safety and adequate supervision, the staff/child ratio should remain constant. Check your state and local licensing requirements for regulations regarding cots, sheets, length of rest periods, removal of children's shoes during rest time, cleaning and sanitation procedures, and other requirements.

Creating the Environment

Provide an unrushed schedule that has appropriate expectations and a balance between active and quiet times to promote rest and relaxation. Each classroom should have a quiet area where a child can go to rest or play alone. Soft washable cushions or soft mats and a sense of privacy make the space more inviting. A view of the child while in the quiet area is needed for supervision.

During rest time, use dim lighting, but it should not be dark. Soothing music may contribute to relaxation, but a radio may be distracting or disruptive to rest because of voice variations. Since water has a calming effect, water fountains, audio recordings of water sounds, and aquariums can enhance the rest time environment. Nonpoisonous plants and soft colors can create a soothing effect.

Provide each child with a cot or mat on which to rest. Place cots to allow easy access while not blocking emergency exit routes. Be sensitive to children's needs and desires when placing cots; for example, some children may have fears that can be alleviated by placing their cots near an adult or near a light. Encourage children to bring a favorite blanket, sheet, or a washable stuffed toy. Provide individual storage spaces for children's blankets and toys.

Evaluation:

☒ Are children role-playing relaxation, rest, and sleep?

☒ Are children talking about their feelings related to rest time and nighttime?

Family Information & Activity Bulletin

I Need My Rest

Children need more sleep than adults. Most young children need 10 to 12 hours of sleep each night and a short nap during the day. Some children resist bedtime and sleep. Often, the more tired they are, the more they try to stay awake. Children will fall asleep more quickly if they have a routine that allows them to relax before bedtime. This may include taking a bath, brushing teeth, reading a story, getting a last drink of water, and lots of hugs.

Some children have difficulty sleeping because of bad dreams or night terrors. These may be caused by seeing or experiencing violence, watching scary television shows, or hearing adults talk about frightening events. Even children's stories and fairy tales can frighten some children. Nightmares are very real to a child. If you know what frightens your child, you can probably prevent some bad dreams in the future.

Family Activities

☒ Talk about why rest and sleep are important and what happens when family members get tired.

☒ With suggestions from your child, develop a bedtime routine. Establish a time to begin the routine each night so your child will get enough rest.

Ideas Please

☒ Give us your ideas for stories or activities that help your child relax, rest, or sleep.

Items Please

☒ Send the class pictures of people or animals sleeping.

Children's Activities

Pillow Talk

Before the activity, select throw pillows. To begin the activity, place pillows throughout the area and encourage children to explore. Once children have had the opportunity to see and feel the pillows, ask open-ended questions like, "What do you think about the pillows?" Share with the children that pillows provide comfort. Explain that everyone needs rest and that there are many ways, times, and places where people rest. Tell everyone to use the pillows to get comfortable and rest. Play the instrumental version of "Voyage for Dreamers" while the children rest. Leave a few pillows out and tell children they can use them to rest whenever they need one.

Materials

a variety of washable pillows (many sizes, shapes, colors, textures, levels of firmness, patterns, with removable covers and permanent covers), instrumental version of "Voyage for Dreamers," by Pamala Ballingham (*Voyage for Dreamers*. Earth Mother, 03).

Other Ideas

- Give each child a pillowcase to decorate in any way he or she chooses.
- Visit a store that sells linens and look at all the different kinds of pillows, sheets, pillowcases, bedspreads, mattress covers, blankets, and quilts.
- Visit a music store and listen to soft music.
- Interview a band director and ask how they let the musicians know when to play softly.
- Visit furniture or mattress stores to see many kinds of beds. Look for different sizes.
- Read *No Nap,* by Eve Bunting (New York: Clarion, 1989).

In and Out

Blow up a beach ball. Show children how you breathe in and then blow air out of your lungs and into the beach ball. Let them feel the air as it escapes the beach ball.

Guide children to breathe in slowly and breathe out through their mouths. Tell them to feel the air flow out of their mouths with their hands. Encourage them to take longer and deeper breaths and to exhale completely. Make a soft, sighing sound while exhaling, and see if they can too. Next, invite children to stretch up as they inhale and bend down as they exhale.

Materials

beach ball

Other Ideas

- Visit a yoga class and talk to students about breathing.
- Invite a yoga instructor to introduce breathing and stretching to the class.
- Ask a voice teacher to demonstrate breathing and explain the importance.
- Visit a choir practice and ask about breathing.

Body Work

Ask children if they ever rub a place that hurts to make it feel better. Explain that massage therapists help other people relax, rest, and feel better by stretching and rubbing the other person's muscles and joints. Have children use one of their hands to massage the other hand. Then encourage children to use both hands and massage their own legs and feet. Let children choose to massage one another's feet. Show children some massage tools designed for home use. Have children predict how it would feel to use the different tools, and then let the children try using the tools.

Materials

massaging sandals, vibrating pillows, massaging shower head, footbath massager, massage balls of various types, car seat massager, handheld body massager

Other Ideas

- Visit a massage therapist to see the office and ask questions about massage therapy.
- Visit stores that sell massage tools.
- Let children soak their feet in individual washtubs or bowls of warm water and two drops of lavender oil.

Dancing Light

With the lights dimmed, announce to the children that you want them to make light "dance." Tell them that you are going to turn out the lights and play some music while they make the light from their flashlights dance on the ceiling, walls, and floor. Have each child get a throw pillow and a flashlight and find a place on the floor to rest. Play "Sky Dances," by Holly Near. After the song, turn the lights on and have children return their pillows and flashlights. Discuss the dancing lights.

Materials
throw pillows, flashlights, tape or CD, tape or CD player, "Sky Dances," by Holly Near (*Sky Dances.* Redwood Records, 8902).

Other Ideas
- Visit a store that sells lights to see many flashlights and find out which type sells the most.
- Add transparent colored film or paper to the flashlights to create colored lights.
- Attend a light show or fireworks display.
- Visit a live performance theater to see the lighting and talk with lighting technicians.

Glow Show
Ask the children if they have seen anything glow in the dark, and listen to their experiences. Tell them you have some things that glow in the dark and will let them use them to create a poster. Have them talk about what they might create. Support children as they create. After all posters are finished and dry, have a special "Glow Show." Let children work on invitations that will glow in the dark, and send them to another class or their families. Also invite local media to the event.

Until the show, let children place their posters where they can see them whenever they rest. Have children hold posters so that all guests can see. Ask visitors to remain seated and turn the lights off for one minute. When the lights are turned back on, invite guests to walk around and ask the artists questions. Let children take their posters home to look at when they rest there.

Materials
glow-in-the-dark supplies or objects (paint, chalk, stars, stickers), poster board, glue, tissue paper, glitter

Other Ideas
- Visit a store to look for glow-in-the-dark products.
- Visit a bookstore or library to see the bedtime story books, as well as books about pillows, light, dark, nighttime, stars, resting, soft sounds, dreams, and beds.

Chapter 3

Foods I Eat

One way young children explore their world is through tasting and putting things in their mouths. Learning about and experiencing foods can be a fun topic for children, staff, and families.

Distinguishing between what should and should not go in the mouth can be introduced in a positive manner by allowing children to choose and try many foods. As the children learn about things they don't enjoy tasting, teachers can introduce the idea that, just as they *choose* not to put certain foods in their mouth, they *need* to keep certain harmful objects and substances away from their mouths.

Involving families in this theme is an ideal way to expose children to a wide variety of interesting foods. As children begin to learn about the various ways that food is prepared and the methods used to serve meals, other topics can be introduced. It is important that children know how to share food without spreading germs, how food helps the body, and what things go in the mouth.

Addressing Diversity

Food preference is largely determined by family and experiences. In addition, who prepares food and the role children have at mealtime will vary depending on the family and culture. Consideration of family, cultural, and religious food values and traditions is important in planning food activities. Also take into consideration allergies and individual taste preferences.

Planning activities so that all children can relate to some of them provides a model of inclusion and allows everyone to learn from one another. Showing respect for cultural, religious, family, and individual needs and interests will enhance the food theme.

Where Will the Theme Lead?

Use these words to stimulate ideas for follow-up activities:

hungry	canned	fast food	condiments	diet
flavors	recipes	camp fire	harvest	dishes
fruits	ice cream	cafeteria	traditions	pet food
vegetarian	wok	rice	cuisine	disposal
crunchy	tortilla	chef	poison	allergies

Learning Center Materials

Dramatic Play:
empty food containers
centerpiece, tablecloths, napkin rings
empty, labeled spice containers
coupons, play money
paper pad for taking orders
green beans to string and snap
edible herbs (mint, lemon grass, etc.)
tongs
pot holder
cookbook, recipes, recipe holder

Table Toys:
food puzzles
plastic fruit to sort and match to pictures
lotto and domino games that feature food
seed packets to sort
dry beans to sort
different spice containers and lids
containers of pet food for matching
containers of seeds for matching
puzzles of plants and foods

Language Arts:
computer software about
  food digestion
gardening magazines
cooking magazines
food and grocery store advertisements
restaurant advertisements
menus
seed catalogs
video of a TV cooking show
videos of class food experiences
resource books with germ information

Science:
pictures of digestion
raw food to handle and observe change
  (potato peels, slice of raw potato, bread,
  slice of apple)
various sizes of apples and scales
carrot, turnip, or mint plant
spices to taste
seed collection
pet food containers
pot holder-making kit

Blocks:
catalog of kitchen furniture
plastic food to haul in trucks
toy pots and pans for hauling
large seeds for hauling (peach pits,
  avocado seeds)
clean, empty food boxes
cans
milk and juice containers
artificial aquarium plants
pictures of restaurants and groceries

Art:
food magazines
food container labels
restaurant coupons
restaurant advertisements
food stickers
straws
pottery clay
nontoxic berries to make dye
seeds for making mosaics
centerpieces

Outdoors:
water cooler and cups
picnic table or plastic tablecloth
shovel
rake
plant and tree field guides
magnifying glasses
trash bag or can
work gloves
containers for collecting seeds
disconnected section of water hose

Library Books:
Eating Out, by Helen Oxenbury
  (New York: Dial, 1983).
*Daddy Makes the Best
  Spaghetti,* by Anna Grossnickle Hines (New
  York: Clarion, 1986).
This Is the Way We Eat Our Lunch, by Edith
  Baer (New York: Scholastic, 1995).
Everybody Cooks Rice, by Norah Dooley
  (Minneapolis: Carolrhoda, 1991).
D.W. The Picky Eater, by Marc Brown (New
  York: Little Brown, 1995).

Topic 1
When I'm Hungry

Learning Objectives:

☑ Children will state ways they know they are hungry (i.e., stomach growls, feels empty).

☑ Children will stop eating when they are full.

☑ Children will state that the body needs food.

Children begin to develop food associations and eating habits in infancy. When infants are hungry, they cry. The result is usually that they are fed and their hunger is alleviated. Further, they learn that, by crying, they not only receive food and feel better, but develop feelings of security while being held and cuddled.

As children grow, they can learn to recognize specific needs and distinguish between feelings like being hungry and needing food or being sad and needing a hug. Promote the idea that food is for hunger rather than for reward or comfort.

For most young children, hunger occurs about every three hours. They have small stomachs that cannot hold as much food as an adult's stomach. Offer nutritious, appetizing choices of food in small portions, and then encourage the children to eat until they are full. Forcing children to clean their plates encourages overeating.

Since most children will naturally select sweet foods and desserts first, teachers may want to limit desserts until after other foods have been tasted. This does not mean children must eat everything on their plates, but they should try different foods and eat at least a portion of their other food. It's okay for children to "save room" for dessert!

Young children cannot begin to understand the digestive process, but they can begin to understand that their bodies need food and water. Many children may find it fascinating to be introduced to what happens to food after it is swallowed.

Creating the Environment

The ideal environment would provide children with a variety of nutritious, appetizing choices of food. Meals that allow children to select the food and serve themselves may help encourage children to try new foods and begin to take responsibility for their food choices. Provide assistance as necessary to help children choose appropriate-sized portions.

Child-sized tables and chairs let young children easily reach the table while sitting comfortably with feet touching the floor. Small trays, plates, and cups make it easier for children to grasp, lift, and carry.

Encourage a "home-like" environment by involving children in passing serving bowls and serving themselves. Teachers and children may occasionally use place mats, tablecloths, centerpieces, or napkins to make the table setting attractive and to show children examples of different table settings.

Evaluation:

☒ Are children talking about what being hungry feels like?

☒ Do children stop eating when full?

☒ Are words like *hungry* and *full* used during play?

☒ Do children ask questions about how the body uses food?

Family Information & Activity Bulletin

When I'm Hungry

Children need breakfast to get through the busy morning. After all, it has been 10 or 12 hours since their last meal. Skipping breakfast can mean a growling stomach or a grumpy child, making it difficult to do well in school.

Most young children need to eat about every 3 hours. Give them small, nutritious snacks between meals, such as fruit or peanut butter and crackers. It is okay to occasionally give sweets like cookies or cake if your child has eaten healthy foods during meals.

Small children need small servings of food (about 1/4 cup per serving). If children are served large portions of food and forced to clean their plates, they may become overweight or learn to dislike some foods.

Family Activities

- ☒ Have a family discussion about why everyone eats.
- ☒ Provide nutritious, simple-to-fix foods for your child to prepare and eat when hungry.
- ☒ Provide a plastic cup or an individual water bottle for your child to get his or her own drink of water when thirsty.

Ideas Please

- ☒ Give us ideas for field trips and speakers that can help children learn about food and hunger.
- ☒ Suggest songs about food.

Items Please

- ☒ Send the class magazines or catalogs with pictures of food and people eating.
- ☒ Send recipes from magazines and clean, empty food containers and labels.

Children's Activities

What Does *Hungry* Mean?

Introduce children to a doll named Rosita, and tell them that she is hungry. Ask what *hungry* means and what Rosita should do. Hold up a children's dictionary and read what it says about *hungry*. Encourage children to share what it's like to be hungry. Explain that everyone gets hungry sometimes and that it is important to eat when you are hungry. End the activity by saying that you are going to put Rosita in the dramatic play area where the children can feed her and her friends.

Materials
female doll, children's dictionary

Other Ideas

• Encourage children to write a poem about being hungry.

• Let children act out being hungry.

• Interview a veterinarian or pet owner to find out how animals show that they are hungry.

The Lion's Roar

Show the children a stuffed animal or picture of a lion and play a tape of a lion roaring. Ask what else roars or growls. Help them think of other animals, such as dogs, tigers, and bears. Ask the children to roar or growl. Then ask if they have ever heard their stomachs growl. Point out that they may be hungry when their stomachs growls. Say, "Sometimes the stomach muscles start to move at the time you usually eat, even if you haven't eaten yet. The movement sounds like a growl or rumble." Tell them to listen to their stomachs and other people's stomachs for growls.

Safety Note: Check the stuffed animal to ensure that there are no loose parts that children could dislodge, insert in their mouths, and choke on.

Materials
lion picture or stuffed lion, tape of roar sound, tape player

Other Ideas

• Let children interview children in another class about hunger.

• Visit a restaurant and observe behaviors of hungry people.

• Read *Dinosaur Roar!* by Paul and Henrietta Strickland (New York: Dutton, 1994).

Full to the Top

Provide the children with sand and a variety of containers. Invite the children to put sand into the containers. Have them fill some containers so full that they cannot be moved without spilling sand. Then ask the children to explain how they feel after they have eaten. Ask if they know what it feels like to eat too much. Explain that it is important to eat until they feel full, but not so full that they get a stomachache. As follow-up, talk with children about this again after the next time they eat.

Materials

sand, sand scoop, plastic cups, bottles, pitchers, buckets, bowls

Other Ideas

- Ask the children to tell about the foods they eat at home and help them look for food containers and pictures of these foods.

- Visit a grocery store, farmers' market, or another place groceries are purchased.

- Visit a farm, orchard, berry or pumpkin patch to see food growing and do some picking.

- Read *The Gas We Pass: The Story of Farts*, by Shinta Cho (Brooklyn, NY: Kane/Miller, 1994).

Where Does Food Go?

Ask the children where food goes and what happens to it after they eat. Listen to their ideas and write them down. After the children wash their hands, give them soft foods to feel, like bananas and bread. Ask what their teeth do to food when they eat. Cut the food into small pieces like their teeth would. Move the cut-up food into a blender or food processor.

Prepare the children for the noise, then turn on the blender. Add water, if necessary, to mix the food. After the food is mashed, ask the children what happened. Pour mashed food into a bowl so they can see that it is no longer solid. Tell children that when they chew their food, it mixes with saliva. After swallowing, it goes to the stomach, where muscles begin to mash it up (like the food in the blender). Then the food is sent out to feed the rest of the body. Tell them the body uses all it needs and gets rid of the rest of the food when we go to the bathroom. Show children computer simulations, pictures, or a video of the digestive system. As follow-up, invite children in small groups to look up digestion in resource books and on the computer.

Materials

fruits, raw vegetables, blender or food processor, plastic or table knives, digestion resource books, computer, medical and encyclopedia software, digestion videotapes, VCR and monitor.

Other Ideas

- Visit a doctor to learn more about digestion.
- Visit a sanitary landfill (dump) and watch the trash compactor.
- Read *Everyone Poops,* by Taro Gomi (Brooklyn, NY: Kane/Miller, 1993).

Tell Rosita

Introduce the children to a doll named Rosita and some of her friends (other dolls). Be sure to include both male and female dolls, as well as dolls representing different ethnic backgrounds. Tell the children that Rosita and her friends have some questions about food. One at a time, take a card from each doll and read a question to determine what children know about food and hunger. Some examples of questions are: What does *hungry* mean? How do you know if you are hungry? Why do people eat? What does *thirsty* mean? What should you do if you are hungry or thirsty? How much water do our bodies have inside? What happens to food when we swallow it? When should we stop eating?

Materials

dolls, questions on cards

Other Ideas

- Encourage children to write a book about food.
- Let children write a song about food.
- Ask children to collect food pictures and make a scrapbook.

Topic 2
Many Different Foods

Learning Objectives:

☑ Children will sort foods into different food groups.

☑ Children will name foods they eat.

☑ Children will identify foods that give their bodies more of what they need to grow and develop.

☑ Children will taste new foods when offered.

☑ Children will show respect for family and cultural food patterns.

Young children cannot be expected to understand or correctly identify foods in the four food groups or the food pyramid. Children may create their own food groups along traditional lines (vegetables, fruits, sweets, or meats) or by other characteristics, such as color, texture, and preparation method.

Encourage but do not force children to try a variety of foods. The way foods are prepared and served affects the way children feel about certain foods. Foods that are familiar, look and smell good, and served in child-sized portions are more appetizing.

Children may dislike a food at one time and several weeks later decide they like that food, or vice versa. Since children have more taste buds than adults, they are more sensitive to flavors. Foods with pepper or other spices may taste too hot or spicy for young children. Their food likes and dislikes may change as they grow older and the number of taste buds decreases.

Staff need to be aware of children's food allergies. Allergies can cause reactions including moodiness, stomach distress, and hives. Some food reactions may be life-threatening. A child who is severely allergic to a food such as peanuts may go into anaphylactic shock if exposed to peanuts, peanut butter, snack cakes or cookies with peanuts or peanut oil, or even vegetables stir-fried in peanut oil. Find out what type of reaction a child with allergies may have and the specific food or food group that causes the reaction. Those ingredients must be avoided.

As children are exposed to new foods, they may begin to recognize and identify specific foods, first by color and later by food type. For example, broccoli or green beans may be categorized as "green foods" and later as "vegetables." As children begin to understand the concepts of food identification and categorizing, teachers may begin to discuss how specific foods help our bodies. It is essential that children—and adults—recognize that there are no bad foods, but that various foods help our bodies in different ways. Encourage eating a variety of foods to obtain adequate nutrients for growth and development. Children may better understand the overall benefit of food in terms of it helping them grow, giving them energy to run and play, and helping them become strong.

Creating the Environment

Classroom cooking activities provide excellent opportunities to introduce new foods. Follow sound safety and sanitation practices when using appliances and preparing food. You'll need sturdy, clean surfaces for food preparation and adequate storage for appliances not in use. A supply of aprons, pot holders, stirring spoons, measuring spoons and cups, and disposable utensils provide a means for children to be directly involved in preparations.

Evaluation:

☒ Are children sorting and naming foods during play?

☒ Are children talking about foods that help their bodies?

☒ Are children tasting new foods?

Family Information & Activity

Bulletin

Many Different Foods

Food preferences are learned. Most young children do not really like or dislike a food until they try it several times. Encourage your child to try new foods. Start with one or two bites of a new food. If your child doesn't like it, try it again another day. Since children have more taste buds than adults, they are more sensitive to flavors. Foods with pepper or other spices may taste too hot or spicy for young children. Never force children to eat. By letting them stop eating when they are full, you are helping them develop good eating habits.

Family Activity

☒ Help your child make a book about your family and the food you eat. The book can include pictures that family members draw, photographs of food-related activities, labels from food containers, recipes, special celebration menus, and stories told or written by family members. Paste the items onto paper. Sew the pages together, or fasten them using tape, staples, glue, binders, or a folder. Make book covers from illustrations, photographs, food labels, or cloth that is meaningful to the family. Let your child share the book with the class.

Ideas Please

☒ Suggest restaurants or grocery stores to visit that have the foods your family enjoys.

☒ Let us know what kinds of vegetables, breads, and herbs you eat at home.

Items Please

☒ Send the class pot holders, pots, and cooking utensils to add to the dramatic play area.

☒ Send empty, clean food containers, labels, spice containers, and recipes from magazines.

Children's Activities

Lots of Bread

Ask the children to recall and talk about any bread-baking experience they have had. Provide a tray of various breads that children can sample after they wash their hands. Consider including tortillas, pita bread, lefse, and focaccia. Show children the container and the label from each kind of bread. Read *Bread, Bread, Bread*, by Ann Morris, and talk about it with the children. Let the children talk about the kinds of bread they eat at home. Point out that there are many kinds of bread, and that bread is only one kind of food. Ask them to name as many kinds of food as they can think of for you to write down in a book. As they think of other foods they will let you know. Help them write it in the book. Place the class book in the art center for children to illustrate and add to as they want. Place *Bread, Bread, Bread* in the library or dramatic play area.

Materials

wide variety of bread, tray, bread labels and containers, paper, marker, *Bread, Bread, Bread*, by Ann Morris (New York: Lothrop, 1989)

Other Ideas

- Visit a farm to see how food is grown.
- Visit a cannery or other factory where food is prepared.
- Visit a bakery to study food preparation.
- Visit the produce section of a grocery store.
- Visit or invite a basket maker to demonstrate how baskets are made and the significance of baskets.
- Visit a pottery store and ask how pottery is used with food.

Restaurant Visits

Arrange to take small groups of children to visit different kinds of restaurants. Tell the children about the restaurant they will visit and show pictures, menus, advertisements, place mats, or coupons. Show a map with the restaurant marked and the roads to get there highlighted. Help children decide on questions to ask and things to observe. During the visit, children can look at the menu, notice table arrangements, interview staff, take a tour of the kitchen, see machines and tools that are used, sample food, assist workers with tasks, and observe customers. Request a menu and any other material to enhance reporting and role-playing. Use a camera to capture the experience. A take-out food order can be taken back for other children, groups, or classes. After the visits, assist each group in preparing information to share with the other children. To extend the experience, assist children in creating a restaurant in the dramatic play area. Invite the local media to go on the trips or attend the presentations made by children.

Materials
menus, coupons, place mats, pictures, advertisements, map, camera, video camera, film, prepared interview questions

Other Ideas
- Visit a hotel and see the banquet hall and kitchens.
- Show menus and pictures of menu boards, and then let children tell about experiences eating out.
- Invite restaurant owners or employees to visit and tell about their jobs.

Who's the Cook?
Wear an apron and chef hat. If the children have visited restaurants, ask them if they saw any of the cooks. Tell them that cooks work in restaurants but people also cook at home. Ask children who does the cooking in their home and what they cook. Keep a list of the answers children share with the group. Reinforce acceptance of the different people who cook in each of their homes. Help them to see the differences and similarities of the foods they eat. Encourage children to draw a picture of the cooks in their family and display the drawings on a bulletin board. Offer to write on their drawings who the cook is and what they cook.

Materials
apron, chef hat, paper, marker, skin-tone crayons, colored pencils, watercolor crayons, skin-tone construction paper, manila drawing paper

Other Ideas
- Visit a store that sells grills and compare the different kinds.
- Visit the host of a cooking show or invite one as a guest.
- Visit a cooking school or invite a cooking teacher to be a guest.
- Visit a store that sells books about cooking and food.
- Invite family members to visit and cook food for children to sample.
- Provide children with a variety of spices from around the world, both familiar and unfamiliar.
- Invite the school cooks to talk about their jobs.

Limas, Pintos, and Garbanzos

Provide children with containers of uncooked, mixed beans to sort. Tell them that, although they look different, they are all beans. Give children a variety of empty food containers and ask them to tell about the food that comes in them. See how many ways they can sort them. For example, according to color, size, texture, known or unknown, like or dislike, chewy or crunchy, food or drink, hot or cold, vegetable or fruit, cooked or raw, dessert or main course, and soft or hard. Add containers to dramatic play for role-playing.

Safety Note: Red kidney beans are poisonous before cooked. Select beans carefully.

Materials

clean and empty food containers, containers for beans, beans (northern, pinto, large lima, black-eyed, garbanzo, small white, baby lima, green split pea, white kidney, cranberry bean, pink bean, small red, black bean, yellow split pea, lentil, navy, soybean, adzuki)

Other Ideas

- Help children sprout beans.
- Let children examine and sort seeds.
- Provide materials for children to grow a plant that produces food. The children can monitor the care and growth.
- Visit a health food store or cooperative.
- Read *Growing Vegetable Soup*, by Lois Ehlert (San Diego: Harcourt, 1987).
- Play "Jamaica, Jamaica," by Brigadier Jerry (*Reggae for Kids*. RAS, 3095).

Planning a Picnic

Ask children to tell what they know about picnics, and involve them in planning one. Together list all of the things that need to be done to get ready for the picnic. The list might include scheduling, checking weather reports, designing a back-up plan, arranging transportation, making invitations for family and friends, selecting and preparing food, sanitation and hand washing, planning recreation, selecting music, and preparing for clean-up. Small groups of children can work on different jobs. Teachers can support small groups and facilitate planning and the actual picnic event as needed.

Materials

antiseptic wipes, picnic food, paper, marker, calendar, clock, weather report, telephone book, baskets, drinks, cooler and ice, games, trash bags, computer or art materials to develop invitations

Other Ideas

- Invite family members to visit and share with the children some of their family traditions related to food.
- Invite someone who has organized a picnic to tell the class about the experience.
- Plan a picnic for the classroom dolls.

Topic 3
I Share Food, Not Germs

Learning Objectives:

☑ Children will appropriately pass food containers to others.

☑ Children will state how germs are spread by food and beverages.

☑ Children will state or show proper ways and times to share food.

Illnesses and diseases can spread many different ways among children and adults. Potentially harmful germs, bacteria, and viruses travel on food, beverages, and utensils and may cause illness or disease to anyone eating or handling these infected products. To reduce the potential for infection, both children and staff should wash their hands thoroughly before preparing or eating food, both at mealtime and snack time, or when doing classroom cooking activities.

Food storage is also important. Some bacteria, such as staph or salmonella, can multiply in food if left at room temperature for too long. These bacteria can cause food-borne illnesses, which result in severe stomach distress, vomiting, and diarrhea. Foods should be prepared for children just before meal or snack time and served immediately. Leftovers should not remain at room temperature for more than 30 minutes and should be covered and stored in a refrigerator. Staff may contact the local health department for information on cleaning food utensils and proper food preparation and storage.

Staff may want to consider the following issues regarding food sharing:

• Whether to allow children to bring food from home and, if so, how to maintain nutritional balance and meet additional storage requirements

• Whether children are allowed to share food with other children

• What policies need to be set for food that adults provide for the classroom on special occasions

Creating the Environment

The ideal environment would include a refrigerator, paper towels, enough outlets for various appliances, and easy access to a sink. Small bowls used to serve and pass food, serving utensils, and gloves for food preparation are also desirable.

Evaluation:

☒ Do children pass food containers to others upon request?

☒ Are children talking about ways to share food, not germs?

☒ During role-playing, are children sharing food appropriately?

Family Information & Activity Bulletin

I Share Food, not Germs

It's great when children want to share their toys or their cookies, but not when they share germs! Your child should not eat or drink from the same utensils as anyone else, including parents, brothers, or sisters. This can spread germs that cause diseases.

Teach your child to share food the healthy way:

- When sharing a sandwich, apple, or other food, cut first before you take a bite.

- When sharing juice or other drink, first pour it into two glasses.

- Use tongs or serving spoons in food dishes. Don't use a spoon you have had in your mouth.

- When taking food from a platter, take the first item that you touch.

Family Activity

☒ Help your child look around your home for items that shouldn't be shared. Examples include toothbrush, drinking cup, a cookie after someone else takes a bite, and a bag of pretzels (unless everyone who shares washes their hands).

Ideas Please

☒ Tell us what restaurants your family likes that serve buffet style.

Items Please

☒ Pictures of people sharing food would be helpful.

☒ Let your child bring to class boxes, pictures, rags, or anything cut in half.

Children's Activities

Water, Water, Everywhere

Collect a variety of containers (different sizes, lids, spouts). Fill the containers with water and ice, provide the children with cups, and explain that they can get a drink any time they are thirsty. Ask them to tell you what being thirsty feels like and how they will know if they are thirsty. Tell them some people like ice in their water, but others like water at room temperature. Encourage them to try both. Stress that they are to wash their hands first, use a scoop (not their cup) for the ice, and only use their own cup. They can help one another scoop and pour but should not share their cups. Help them write their names on the cups and have them draw on them too. Children who do not recognize their names may remember their drawings. Identify a place to store the cups. Remind them that cups should not touch other cups when they are being stored.

Materials
pitchers with lids, a half gallon jug with a pop-off lid, a gallon jug (half-full), a water cooler with a spout, canteens, hiking/biking water bottles, bottles with squirt lids, other water containers, water, cups, cooler and ice, ice scoop, markers, individual bottles of water with screw-off lids

Other Ideas
- Visit a sports store to see all kinds of water bottles.
- Visit public places to see different drinking fountains and water bottles.

Pass the Peas, Please

Invite a small group of children to role-play a meal with you. Direct children to wash their hands with water and soap and dry them completely with paper towels. Have a variety of containers and serving utensils, as well as a place setting for each child. Use pretend food that children can remove with different utensils. Begin by telling children that the food is for all of them to share, so they will be passing it to one another. Ask them to explain how they can do that without touching the food. Make requests for different dishes from several children and let them practice passing the containers. Let children request foods to be passed to them by other children. Have children identify their own dishes and utensils, and then the ones that will be used by the entire group. Reinforce that individual utensils do not go into the containers used by the group and that the group utensils are for serving food. Allow more time for children to request and pass food and to put some on their plate. Explain that this is a way to share food, not

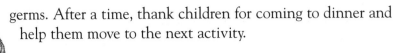

germs. After a time, thank children for coming to dinner and help them move to the next activity.

Materials

plastic bowl with large jingle bells inside, wooden bowl with scraps of wadded paper, deep metal bowl with water inside, ladle, glass bowl with pine cones and water inside, place setting for each child, plastic plate with clay circles on it, spatula, serving spoons, table knife and fork, glass plate with sponges on it, tongs, basket with blocks inside and no serving utensil

Other Ideas

- Have a tea party and pass around sugar and cream.
- Play "The Sharing Song," by Raffi (*Singable Songs for the Very Young*. Shoreline, 10037).

Buffet Bound

Arrange for children to visit a restaurant that serves a buffet. Encourage children to observe the workers and the customers. During the visit, spend time on a kitchen tour and observe the containers and utensils. Facilitate an interview with staff. Ask for a review of the rules about customers eating at the buffet table and any rules for staff. Let children eat and have them practice following the rules. Send a large thank-you note that the children make together to the restaurant staff.

Materials

chart paper, glitter crayons, watercolor crayons, colored pencils

Other Ideas

- Set up a buffet for lunch.
- Invite people who work in a restaurant with a buffet to talk about the rules.
- Invite someone from the health department to explain about restaurant and food inspections.

Half a Cookie

Read *The Very Hungry Caterpillar*, by Eric Carle. Allow time for children to make comments or ask questions about the book. If children do not initiate it, point out that the caterpillar did not eat all the food. Ask children if it would be okay for them to finish the caterpillar's food. Stress that they should not eat leftovers if someone has taken a bite of it. Hold up two paper dolls and a paper cookie. Introduce one paper doll as Jama and one as Omar. Explain that if Jama has a cold and takes a bite of a cookie, and then

Omar takes a bite of the same cookie, Omar will probably get a cold too. Remind them that germs can be spread by sharing drinks and bites of food that someone else has already tasted. Ask how Omar and Jama could share food but not germs. Tell them if they want to share food, it should be before anyone takes a bite. Cut a paper cookie in two and put half by Omar and half by Jama to show how to share.

Materials

two paper dolls, a paper cookie, scissors, *The Very Hungry Caterpillar*, by Eric Carle (New York: Philomel, 1979)

Other Ideas

- Provide the children with playdough and plastic knives to practice cutting.

- Provide bread and table or plastic knives for children to use for cutting practice.

- Read *Give Me Half*, by Stuart J. Murphy (New York: Harper, 1996).

Sharing Food

Involve small groups of children in planning and preparing a snack to be shared by the class. Provide children's cookbooks and recipes for them to review for ideas. Ask many questions to prepare the children for selecting food, buying ingredients, fixing food, and appropriately serving and sharing it without spreading germs. Assist them in determining the amount needed to serve all children. Arrange a trip to the grocery store to purchase food, and assist children as needed in preparing and serving it. Help them clean up after preparing and eating the snack.

Materials

paper, pencils, children's cookbooks, recipes, ingredients (to be identified by children), cooking utensils and dishes (to be identified by children)

Other Ideas

- Provide a selection of food for children to choose from and prepare a snack for the class.

- Involve all children in snack preparation and invite another class to enjoy.

- Involve all children in snack preparation and invite community administrators to enjoy.

Topic 4
For My Mouth

Learning Objectives:

☑ Children will identify food and nonfood.

☑ Children will state what might happen if nonfood items are put into their mouths.

Be aware of the dangers of poisonous substances in the school environment. Some substances, such as toilet cleaner and dishwasher detergent, may contain corrosive chemicals that severely burn the mouth, throat, and stomach in just a few seconds. Products containing petroleum, such as gasoline or turpentine, can cause damage if swallowed or inhaled.

All indoor plants and plants in play areas should be nonpoisonous. It is difficult for young children to differentiate between berries that we eat, such as blackberries or blueberries, and berries that are toxic, such as those on holly or yaupon bushes. Learn the names of plants in your area, then check with your regional poison control center for information on toxicity.

Choking is a hazard with children under age three because they often put toys in their mouths. Be especially careful with balloons. They are one of the greatest choking or smothering hazards for both young and older children. Check all toys for small, broken, or removable parts. Children may also choke on food items and should never run, jump, or play with food, gum, or candy in their mouths. Foods that are hard or round, such as hot dogs, hard candy, grapes, nuts, and popcorn, can also cause choking. Sticky foods, such as a spoonful of peanut butter or raisins, can block the air passage. Check with your area children's hospital or pediatric clinic for more information on preventing choking, and have at least one person trained in first aid and CPR available at all times, including field trips.

Creating the Environment

Keep all potentially toxic items in a locked cabinet, including cleaning solutions, bleach and other disinfectants, rubber cement, and medications. Aerosols, such as room deodorizers, are also toxic.

Prepare foods served to children in a way that prevents choking, such as cutting hot dogs into small squares (not circles), cutting raw vegetables into skinny strips rather than chunks, separating raisins, and serving only a thin layer of peanut butter on crackers. If balloons are to be used, Mylar balloons are suggested.

Evaluation:

☒ Are children talking about the effects of poison and choking?

☒ Are children sorting food and nonfood items during play?

Family Information & Activity Bulletin

For My Mouth

Cleaning supplies, bleach, make-up, medicines, shampoo, and other products typically found in the house can be poisonous if swallowed. Toilet cleaner and dishwasher detergent will cause severe throat and stomach burns. Some drain cleaners are extremely dangerous.

Keep all cleaning fluids away from children. Even if you have safety latches, do not store hazardous supplies under the sink. Many children can open latches. Keep fertilizers and bug sprays in a locked cabinet.

To protect children, always put the top back on containers and put them away after use. Never put poisonous substances in beverage bottles or food containers.

If you think your child has swallowed or breathed something potentially poisonous, call the poison control center immediately. Keep a bottle of syrup of ipecac at home. This medicine, found at drugstores, causes vomiting. Do not give this medicine unless you talk to the poison control center! Some poisons cause even worse problems if a child vomits.

Family Activity
☒ Take a walk with your child and look for things that are edible and things that are not. Encourage your child to ask you questions about what is safe to eat.

Ideas Please
☒ Suggest places we could visit to learn about poison and how to avoid it.

Items Please
☒ We could use washed seeds left over from food and magazines with pictures of animals.

Children's Activities

Table Top

Get input from families and gather a diverse sampling of items other than food that might be on a dinner table. Cover the items with a tablecloth. Tell children to name things that might be on a table where people eat. Draw a line down the middle of a piece of chart paper and write "food" at the top on one side and "not food" on the other. As children name things, ask them to specify if it is food or not. Once they have shared all their ideas, remove the tablecloth and have children check if all foods are listed on the chart. Add to the list if needed. Point out that some items on a dinner table, such as napkins or salt and pepper shakers, aren't food and should not be eaten.

Materials

candlesticks, tablecloths of different materials, place mats of different materials, place cards, flower arrangement, marker, napkins, various dishes, eating utensils, confetti, salt and pepper shakers, decorations, chart paper

Other Ideas

- Visit gift shops likely to have table decorations.
- Visit department stores to see tablecloths, place mats, napkins, and other table-related items.
- Invite families to set up a table display showing how their dinner table looks.
- Read *Feathers for Lunch*, by Lois Ehlert (New York: Harcourt, 1990).

Kitchen Cabinets

Include children in gathering kitchen supplies from the dramatic play area and place them on a tablecloth to examine. Have children group the items many different ways. Ask what else they think their family keeps in the kitchen cabinets. Show them some empty containers of typical poisons kept in kitchens. Stress that poisons can make them sick if they eat or drink them, and that some can burn the skin and hurt. Encourage children to talk to an adult about poisons in their home. Ask children to return supplies to the dramatic play area. Immediately remove all poison containers used in the activity.

Safety Note: Even empty poison containers can be extremely dangerous, especially drain cleaner and dishwasher detergent containers. Clean containers in advance and keep them stored in a locked cabinet. Immediately after the activity, remove containers from children's reach.

Materials

kitchen supplies from the dramatic play area, tablecloth, dishwasher detergent container, mouse bait box, rust remover can, drain opener bottle, bug spray can, bleach bottle

Other Ideas

- Make a display of labels from poison containers.
- Visit a store to see products that may be poisonous.
- Invite a health professional to explain what happens to someone's body if they are poisoned.

Berry Patch

Read *Blueberries for Sal*, by Robert McCloskey, and talk about the story. Let children wash their hands and help prepare blueberry muffins. Tell the children that some berries can be eaten but some others are poisonous, so they should never eat berries until they check with an adult.

Materials

blueberry muffin mix, ingredients noted on box, muffin pan, bowl, spoon, can opener, oven, *Blueberries For Sal*, by Robert McCloskey (New York: Viking, 1948)

Other Ideas

- Visit a cooperative farm supply store or a hardware store to see seeds.
- Visit a nature center to learn about plants and people who study them.
- Serve blueberries alone instead of in blueberry muffins.

Water Walk

Select a site that is near water and good for walking. Provide the children with individual water bottles half-filled with water and help them put their names on them. Inform children that they are going on a walk to see what water they can find. Tell them that they are to carry their water bottles with them because the water they find will not be for drinking. Remind them that only they are to drink from their bottle. Invite them to take paper and pencils to sketch what they see. The teacher could carry a container with paper, pencils, tape measure, camera, and any other tools to enhance the walk. Look for puddles, streams, ponds, rivers, water dishes for pets, birdbaths, or any other water. Discuss each body of water discovered and reinforce that it is not water for people to drink.

Materials
individual water bottle for each child, marker for labeling bottles, paper, pencils, tape measure, camera, film

Other Ideas
- Visit a pet store to see drinking containers for pets.
- Walk on the playground after a rain.

Pet Food
Put small amounts of different pet food into bowls. Let children feel and smell the food and guess what it is. Show them the original containers and let them match the containers to the food. Invite them to tell about any pets they have fed and how they knew what, how much, and when to feed them. After the stories, reinforce that pet food is for pets. Although it is food, it is not for them to eat. Encourage children to create posters about pet food using the food itself, containers, and other art supplies. Follow-up with any child interested in finding out what other animals eat.

Materials
a variety of pet food and the containers they come in (dog food, cat food, fish food, hamster food), catnip, poster board, glue, scissors, pet magazines, colored craft sticks, felt, wood pieces, watercolor markers

Other Ideas
- Visit a pet store to learn about feeding pets and to see pet food.
- Invite a veterinarian to talk about the importance of nutrition for pets.
- Get a classroom pet and do research on what and how to feed it.

Chapter 4

My Mad, Sad, Glad, and Scary Feelings

The purpose of this theme is to help children identify and express feelings at a level appropriate to their language skills and development and to encourage self-awareness and confidence. Each new experience and the resulting feelings can be confusing for a child. As children learn about themselves and explore their surroundings, teachers can support them by providing factual information and by helping them cope with and express their feelings in a positive manner.

As information is obtained by children or provided by teachers, allow time for children to individually process the information and to ask the questions that are most important to them. In this manner, you allow the children to proceed through emotional processes at the rate they are comfortable with, not the rate at which adults may perceive as appropriate.

Activities and resources presented will promote self-confidence, appropriate expression of feelings, increased social skill, and cooperation with others.

Addressing Diversity

An excellent way to help children understand and show acceptance is to focus on the various similarities and differences in the ways in which people celebrate, grieve, and show respect and other emotions in various cultures, religions, and families. By studying how diverse populations and cultures show emotions and feelings, children may begin to exhibit a wider range of emotions and feelings themselves.

Remind children that all people have feelings, but they all express those feelings in very different ways. Even when customs or expressions differ because of culture, language, religion, or family, children can be encouraged to identify the feelings.

Where Will the Theme Lead?

Use these words to stimulate ideas for follow-up activities:

opinion	cooperation	bury	funeral	obituary
emotions	respect	life cycle	zealous	surprised
confident	creepy	sensitive	cemetery	grave
angry	bones	baffled	grouchy	dramatic
laugh	shocked	fascinated	bashful	excited

Learning Center Materials

Dramatic Play:
hand mirrors
full-length mirrors
dolls that cry or laugh
close up pictures of faces
dress up clothes for funeral
boxes to use for caskets
plastic, silk, or dried flowers
tape, record, or CD player
different types of music

Table Toys:
miniature animals
face puzzles
blocks with different textures
dollhouse and dolls
sand or dirt for burying things
small plastic hand trowel or shovel
artificial flowers to arrange
board games
floor puzzles

Language Arts:
flannel board and
  characters
greeting cards
puppets
cassette recorder and blank tapes
books that describe funerals
books that describe death and rituals
flower arrangement books
books and tapes on the life cycles of
  plants and animals
books and tapes about the food chain

Science:
sandpaper and scrap wood
sand and water tables
mud-making supplies
measuring instruments, such as tape
  measures and yard sticks
watering and mixing containers
containers for planting
grow lights
recycling containers
seeds

Blocks:
mirrors
pictures of fun activities
wooden figures
plastic pets
pictures of headstones and markers
plastic flowers for props
plastic farm animals
walkie-talkies
stuffed animals

Art:
modeling clay
textured objects to make
  rubbings
finger paints
wooden hammer
paper bags and socks
playdough-making supplies
plastic, silk, or dried flowers
clean, empty, colored plastic jugs
charcoal, markers, colored chalk

Outdoors:
punching bag
kick balls
water and sand
hammer and wood stumps or logs
musical instruments
work gloves, hard hats
shovels, trowels, rakes, hoes
watering containers
megaphone

Library Books:
*Alexander and the Terrible,
  Horrible, No Good, Very Bad
  Day,* by Judith Viorst, (New
  York: Atheneum, 1972).
Amazing Grace, by Mary Hoffman (New York:
  Dial, 1991).
Big Friend, Little Friend, by Eloise Greenfield
  (New York: Black Butterfly, 1991).
The Tenth Good Thing About Barney, by Judith
  Viorst (New York: Atheneum, 1971).

Topic 1
My Emotions

Learning Objectives:

☑ Children will identify various emotions felt in specific situations.

☑ Children will display acceptable behavior for the expression of various emotions.

☑ Children will cope with situations by exhibiting problem solving.

Planned activities are important for increasing children's understanding of events and the emotions attached to the events; however, helping children express emotions as they occur is most important. Children learn from many types of situations and circumstances. They also learn by watching how teachers act and react. Remember to model emotional expressions in a positive way and use problem-solving skills to determine effective ways of dealing with emotions.

Each day is filled with events that elicit the same feelings (happiness, sadness, surprise, anger, love) in both children and adults. These situations can become learning experiences if adults take time to talk with children about their own feelings and the children's feelings. Another opportunity for discussion occurs when children are expressing various emotions. When children are playing together and smiling, teachers might remark on how happy they look and encourage the children to express how they feel.

When children cry, it could mean they are hurt, sad, angry or afraid. Encourage them to talk about what happened that made them cry, and ask how they feel about what happened.

Some children may not know why they feel a certain way or may not have words to describe feelings. It is helpful for children to participate in activity or play that allows "acting out" or other ways of expressing themselves. Adults can then help children match words with feelings and assist children in strengthening their problem-solving skills.

Creating the Environment

The ideal environment would include a schedule that allows time for discussion and processing, as well as time to exercise and play as outlets for emotional expression. It is important to model listening and acceptance so that children feel comfortable in expressing their feelings. Having a variety of music, art, art supplies, water, and sand encourages self-expression and emotional awareness. These materials, as well as dolls, dress-up clothes, puppets, and other materials, promote exploration of feelings through role-playing.

Evaluation:

☒ Are children talking about how they feel emotionally?

☒ Are children using words to identify feelings?

☒ Do children use problem-solving skills to find ways to express emotions?

☒ Are children working through feelings during role-playing?

Family Information & Activity Bulletin

My Emotions

Children experience most of the same emotions as adults. Though we try, we can't always accurately understand their emotions. For example, a child who loses a loved one may feel confusion more than sadness.

Help children learn words for how they feel, and help them find appropriate ways to show feelings. When children express anger or fright by hitting others or throwing toys, the behavior must be stopped by firm and understanding intervention. When they calm down, talk about what happened that caused them to want to hit or throw, and help them think of alternate ways to express feelings. Remember that children often learn how to express themselves by watching adults.

Family Activities

☒ Encourage your child to share his or her feelings about normal daily events. This will help them better express significant events, crises, or emergencies.

☒ View with your child a picture or videotape of a family event. Come up with descriptions of how each person's face looks and what they might be feeling.

Ideas Please

☒ Tell us about your family's ways of celebrating happy times.

Items Please

☒ If you have music or artwork that is appropriate for young children to hear and see, consider donating it to the class.

Children's Activities

Look At Me

Distribute mirrors that are easy and safe to handle. In small groups, ask the children to look at themselves in the mirror. Encourage them to make faces if they want. Then give them directions to make a happy face, a sad face, and a mad or angry face. After they make each face, ask children to describe what their faces did and how they looked.

Materials
mirrors for each child

Other Ideas

- After viewing themselves in the mirror, ask children to draw or paint what they saw.
- Children can make faces out of clay.
- Let children draw or cut masks from paper sacks.
- Play "Joy To The World," by Roots Radics (*Reggae for Kids*. RAS, 3095).

Look At Us

Ask children to choose a partner, or separate them into groups of two. Have the partners in each group look at each other and make a happy face. Encourage partners to tell each other what their faces looked like. One at a time, suggest other faces to make (mad, sad, bored, scared) and discuss what they saw.

Materials
none

Other Ideas

- Use a large mirror so the entire group can see themselves as they make faces.
- Have partners draw pictures of each other's face showing a variety of emotions.
- Have partners take pictures of each other while making one of the faces.
- Use string and ruler to measure each partner's smile.

- Encourage children to talk about feelings on a tape recorder or videotape.
- Play "If You're Happy," by Tickle Tune Typhoon (*Hug the Earth*. Tickle Tune Typhoon Records).

How Does It Feel?

Have children lay on mats, cushions, carpet, or a comfortable area on the floor and close their eyes. Begin to talk about topics that would cause a range of emotions, such as clouds, puppies, ice cream, a dark night, a cuddly stuffed animal or blanket, a fast ride on the merry-go-round, swinging high in a swing, a favorite but broken toy, looking up at the stars, visiting someone they love and then going home. Have the children visualize the topics. Encourage children to describe how they feel about each. Support and accept differences in feelings that children express.

Materials
comfortable mats, pillows, cushions, blankets, floor covering

Other Ideas
- Play different music and ask children how they feel after each.
- Have children close their eyes and touch different objects and describe how the items made them feel.
- Encourage children to make different sounds and see how it makes them feel.
- Read *William's Doll*, by Charlotte Zolotow (New York: Harper, 1972).

What Makes Me Feel This Way?

Allow children to work alone or in groups to create pictures of things or activities that make them feel happy, sad, angry, frightened, or excited. In large or small groups, have children display and talk about their pictures. Encourage them to tell what is happening in their pictures and how they feel about it. See if children have ideas about what to do when they feel afraid, sad, or mad. Help them think of ideas.

Materials
newsprint, poster board, blank paper, markers, paint, crayons, tape, easels

Other Ideas
- Have children manipulate plastic figures and props to role-play what causes them to feel various ways.
- Have children role-play or create a play about things or activities that make them feel certain emotions.

- Help children keep a journal about their feelings.
- Read *There's a Nightmare in My Closet,* by Mercer Mayer (New York: Dial, 1990).

Dancing with Your Feelings

Play music from various cultures with different beats, words, and paces. Invite a few children to dance to each type of music. Have children who aren't dancing watch those that are and help the teacher make a list of words to describe the dancers and the music.

Materials

newsprint or poster board, marker, music

Other Ideas

- Have some children sing or play different music while others dance.
- Invite children to choose music that makes them happy or sad and dance to it.
- Let some children assist in videotaping children dancing.
- Visit a music store to listen to different kinds of music.
- Read *My Mama Sings,* by Jeanne Whitehouse Peterson (New York: Harper, 1994).

Topic 2
I Like Myself

Learning Objectives:

☑ Children will identify characteristics they like about themselves.

☑ Children will identify skills they have.

☑ Children will show self-confidence by trying new things.

How responsive and accepting adults are with children helps determine if they learn to like or dislike themselves. A key element in working with children is learning to respect their level of capability and effort. Regardless of how long it takes or how recognizable the product, a child may put a great deal of effort and pride into an activity such as completing a puzzle or painting a picture. Help children feel good about themselves and their abilities by giving recognition. Offer smiles, hugs, or words like, "I really like the colors you used!" or "You really worked hard on that!"

As teachers, try to find a balance between accepting current abilities and challenging children to learn and develop new skills. Children will most naturally develop feelings of self-worth and confidence if teachers take time to interact with them, answer questions, provide information, give positive feedback, and supply a variety of opportunities for new experiences.

Maintain an attitude of guidance and feedback when a child exhibits inappropriate behavior. Let children know that it is the action or behavior that is unacceptable, not them. Additionally, assist the child in finding a more appropriate means of expression. Responding in this way allows children to continue feeling accepted and secure enough to try new things and develop new skills.

Creating the Environment

Hang mirrors and pictures of children at their eye level. Display children's artwork and projects. Include both quiet and busy learning centers and a variety of activities that allow children with different abilities and interests to succeed.

Allow children to choose the learning center they wish to visit and be sure to include materials that reflect each child's race and cultural background. As time passes, add materials based on the interests children show and materials that will provide different challenges and allow success as children develop.

Evaluation:

☒ Do children seem to like themselves?

☒ Do children talk about what they can do?

☒ Do children try new things?

Family Information & Activity

Bulletin

I Like Myself

Children who feel good about themselves are better able to cope with daily situations. Children develop self-esteem by receiving praise and encouragement from parents and through love and security provided at home.

No child excels at everything. Some children can run fast or jump high, others easily learn to read or write, and some can tie their own shoes at an early age. Help your child understand that it's okay if they can't do something. Usually practice will improve or develop skills. Praise children for those skills they have developed and for their efforts to learn new skills. Acknowledge their accomplishments, such as putting away a toy, getting dressed, throwing a ball, or reading or looking through a book with you. Also, let your child know it's okay to make mistakes. Adults make mistakes too.

Family Activity

☒ In front of a mirror, have your child repeat affirmations like, "My favorite thing about me is (my hair, my smile, how smart I am)," and "I sure can (whistle, draw, skip) well."

☒ Let your child choose an activity in which you or the whole family will participate. Let the child be the leader or teacher for the activity.

Ideas Please

☒ Tell us about ways that your family show one another respect or compliments one another.

Items Please

☒ Send the class mirrors that are no longer used and that are in good repair.

Children's Activities

I Can Do This

Have children think of some activity they really like to do or that they think they do well. Ask the children to draw, demonstrate, or talk about the thing they like to do. They can display their picture for the group to see, show the group something they do well, teach the class how to do something, or talk to the group about something they can do. Encourage the group to show appreciation and acceptance of each thing a child contributes.

Materials

markers, crayons, poster board, paper, props children need for their demonstrations

Other Ideas

- Make sharing special things, skills, and ideas with one another a regular classroom activity.
- Invite family members to visit and tell about something they do or their child does well.
- Read *I Like Me!* by Nancy L. Carlson (New York: Viking, 1988).
- Read *I Make Music*, by Eloise Greenfield (New York: Black Butterfly, 1991).
- Play "I'm Never Afraid," by Bonnie Raitt (*Free To Be…A Family.* A&M, 5196).

Talent Show

Have each child choose one special skill or talent to present in a show for parents, another classroom, or other groups of people. Help children identify a wide range of skills they may have, including drawing, running, using a computer, building with blocks, making up songs or stories, and using a hammer. Allow children to arrange space, make invitations, practice their talents, make props, or design costumes for the show. Invite local media to attend.

Materials

props and costumes, music, space for staging the show, paper, markers, paint, signs

Other Ideas

- Divide the class into small groups and let each group stage a talent show, with the other children serving as the audience.
- Invite school and community leaders to visit and show their talent.
- Invite family members to come and perform for the class.
- Read *Gina*, by Bernard Waber (Boston: Houghton, 1995).

"About Me" Display

Designate a space in the classroom for each child to set up a display. It might include their favorite things, drawings or pictures of themselves, pictures of their homes and families, and things that are important to them. Allow the child to add to the display for several days. At the end of that time, each child could make an invitation for someone to come and view their "About Me" display.

Materials

markers, poster board, favorite items, designated space for each child

Other Ideas

- Collect boxes of similar size to let children make an "About Me" box.
- Videotape the children talking about or explaining items in their "About Me" display or box and let them invite people to see the video.
- Do research and make a class display about a famous person.
- Visit a museum to see displays about people.
- Read *All About You*, by Catherine and Laurence Anholt (New York: Viking, 1992).
- Play "Yourself Belongs to You," by The Fat Boys (*Free To Be…A Family*. A&M, 5196).

I'm a Leader

Allow children to take turns being the leader during various transition times and activities. As leader, they might start the activity, decide when to end the activity, or decide how things should be done, arranged, or handled. They might also lead a line, procession, song, or game.

Materials

bell or musical instrument to signal a beginning or ending of an activity, prop to make the leader look or feel special (baton, crown, cape)

Other Ideas

- Have a different "special helper" each day.
- Have each child be leader on an assigned day.
- Invite leaders from school or community to talk about their jobs.
- Read *A Day's Work,* by Eve Bunting (New York: Clarion, 1994).

My Favorites

Designate a "My Favorites" day for each child. On the designated day, allow the child to bring a favorite toy, wear a favorite article of clothing, have a favorite story read, lead a favorite game, and sit in a favorite spot. Encourage discussion about why the child likes these things and show appreciation and support for them.

Materials

materials identified by children

Other Ideas

- Have a "My Favorite" clothes day where all children wear their favorite outfit.
- Have a "My Favorite" day that designates a category (toy, game, book, or music) when all children get to bring their favorite items.
- Let children select their favorite toy at school and tell why.

Topic 3
I Have Many Different Friends

Learning Objectives:

☑ Children will identify individuals who are their friends.

☑ Children will state words that show courtesy and respect.

☑ Children will practice courteous behavior with other children and adults.

Quite often children experience feelings of friendliness before they have words to describe or encourage that friendship. Early on a child may simply play alongside another. Even as children begin to interact more, they still need opportunities to play alone, alongside, and with others.

Friendships for young children may come and go quickly based on the situation at the moment. Encourage children to respect others as they begin to form friendships. Tell them that one way to show respect is by behaving courteously. Guiding children to use words such as "please," "thank you," "you're welcome," "excuse me," and "I'm sorry," helps them learn to respect other people.

As teachers model and guide the use of respectful language and behavior, they should make sure their expectations for children are culturally and developmentally appropriate. Behaviors that are hurtful, discriminatory, or unfair to others should be stopped and an explanation given of why the behaviors hurt people.

Creating the Environment

The ideal environment would include time to play together and alone and some freedom for children to sit by who they want and where they want. Materials and equipment to promote socialization might include a double slide, a trike with a double seat, and art and woodworking materials to make items for friends. Activities should include and encourage communication and cooperation between children.

Evaluation:

☒ Are children playing with others peacefully?

☒ Do children use courtesy words?

☒ Are children showing acceptance of differences in others?

Family Information & Activity Bulletin

I Have Many Different Friends

Some children are outgoing and make friends easily. Other children are more comfortable by themselves or with just one or two other children. Talk with your child about being a friend, and ask who their friends are. It's okay for children to have best friends or ones they enjoy playing with most.

It's not uncommon for a child to say "No one likes me." When children say this, they may feel that way at the moment. Try to find out why they feel that way. It could be that another child has hurt their feelings. Or it might be that the child is shy and doesn't know how to talk or play with other children yet. Discuss how to be a friend to others.

Family Activities

- ☒ Find pictures in magazines of children or adults doing things together and talk about all the things friends might do together.
- ☒ Read a book to your child about friendship and discuss why friends like each other.

Ideas Please

- ☒ Give us ideas about field trips, activities, and guest speakers that would help your child practice or learn social skills, explore friendships, or promote a cooperative spirit.
- ☒ Tell us about your child's and your family's friendships.

Items Please

- ☒ Send empty shoeboxes to the classroom.
- ☒ We could use pictures from sources like magazines and junk mail showing children playing or working together.

Children's Activities

What I Like To Do With My Friends

Encourage children to contribute to a classroom mural about friendships. Children can draw or paint a picture of themselves and friends doing something they like to do. They can also cut and paste pictures of things they like to do with friends. During group time, have children tell about their contributions to the mural.

Materials

large sheet of paper, markers, crayons, colored pencils, paint, scissors, glue, magazines

Other Ideas

- Have children tell about an activity they like to do with friends.
- Encourage children to make a song or listen to songs about friendship.
- Let children create a book about friendship.
- Read *Margaret and Margarita*, by Lynn Reiser (New York: Greenwillow, 1993).
- Play "My Buddy," by Amy Grant (*For Our Children*. Disney, 60616).

Working Together

Develop a chart for daily classroom chores. Each day, invite children to form teams or partnerships. Ask each team or partnership to choose a different classroom chore to work on together. After completing their daily chore, they can add a mark, star, or other designation to the chart.

Materials

a reusable "chores chart" (laminated, chalkboard, or magnetic board), markers for chart (chalk, stars, ink markers)

Other Ideas

- Develop a chart for outside/playground chores.
- Have teams or partnerships responsible for the same chore for an entire week.

- Have pairs of children carry a large ball from one place to another.
- Have children develop a book about working together.
- Read *The Little Red Hen,* by Byron Barton (New York: Harper, 1993).

Mealtime

Role-play a sit-down meal. Have children practice setting the table, serving food, saying "please" and "thank you," and cleaning up after the meal.

Materials

tables and chairs, plates, cups, glasses, forks, spoons, serving bowls, napkins, trays

Other Ideas

- Practice helping and courtesy words at a real meal or snack.
- Role-play preparing and serving a meal, emphasizing cooperation, helpfulness, and appropriate expressions of appreciation.
- Plan a cooking activity that involves cooperation.
- Read *Manners,* by Aliki (New York: Greenwillow, 1990).
- Play "Use A Word," by Red Grammar (*Teaching Peace.* Children's Group, 4202).

Games We Play

Ask children to divide into teams or use an activity to divide them. Encourage each group to make up a new game or to find a different way to play a game they already know. Support teams by asking questions, recording ideas, and providing needed materials. The only rule teams must follow is to make sure everyone is included in some way. Watch for children to use appropriate expressions of support, encouragement, and respect for their team members.

Materials

materials identified by children

Other Ideas

- Take a traditional game and ask each group to decide on a new feature to add.
- Have each group demonstrate and teach their new game to the large group.
- Play games from different countries.
- Read *Rainbow Fish to the Rescue,* by Marcus Pfister (New York: North-South, 1995).

Bring a Friend Day

Ask children to think about someone outside of the classroom who is their friend. Set aside a couple days during the month for children to invite friends to the classroom. Work with parents to make this successful. Have children make invitations and practice verbally inviting the friend. Assist them as necessary to mail the invitation or prepare it for hand delivery. Invitations should include an RSVP to the teacher. Let each child involved know when an RSVP is received. Help children practice making introductions and then allow the children to introduce their friends and tell something about them.

Materials
paper, markers, crayons, envelopes, stamps

Other Ideas

- Challenge children to make a new friend during an outing or joint activity with another class. The new friend could be invited to the classroom and introduced.

- Allow children to bring their pet "friends" to class.

- Have children bring pictures of friends they have.

- Invite a family member to come and talk about family friends and what they do together.

- Play "Rapp Song," by Red Grammar (*Teaching Peace*. Children's Group, 4202)

Topic 4

When Someone or Something Dies

Learning Objectives:

☑ Children will use terms related to death, dying, and ceremonies surrounding death.

☑ Children will express emotions and feelings related to death experiences.

☑ Children will become familiar with various death rituals.

☑ Children will show respect for death rituals that are unfamiliar.

☑ Children will begin exploring the interconnectedness of life and death.

Introduce this topic by giving examples of real experiences that teachers, children, or families have had, or use examples from nature. Since various religions, cultures, and families have different rituals and beliefs surrounding death, it is best to explore a variety of terms, rituals, and emotions so that you do not inadvertently promote the ideas of any group over another.

Concentrate on gathering and providing information on death customs of the cultures and families represented in the classroom. It is helpful, however, to include information from cultures not represented, giving children a broader understanding as they interact with other people.

Provide ample opportunity for children to ask questions. Answer honestly, but if you don't have an answer, explain that you don't know and involve children in research to find possible answers. You might also ask children what they think instead of trying to provide answers yourself. Facilitate discussion by reading books on the topic aloud, listening to music that deals with the topic, inviting guests to share information, allowing children to talk about their experiences in a group, and by observing nature.

Creating the Environment

Include books and music that deal with some aspect of death, or music that might be used during various death rituals. Provide materials in activity centers that promote role-playing of rituals or ceremonies.

To see the processes involved and the connection between life and death, it would be beneficial to have an area either inside or out that is devoted to growing things. If space is not available, use nature walks, field trips, and books to explore the life cycle of various plants, trees, animals, and birds that might be found in your area.

Evaluation:

☒ Do children talk about death and use related words?

☒ Are children role-playing about death?

☒ Do children show respect for death rituals unfamiliar to them?

Family Information & Activity

Bulletin

When Someone or Something Dies

Death of a loved one, a classmate, or even a pet can be traumatic. Children often have difficulty understanding death and the rituals associated with it. When a person or pet dies, your child may have various emotions, depending upon age and development and upon how close your child was to the person or animal. A child may be sad, angry, scared, or confused. Sometimes children seem unconcerned or even happy. Children do not always have the same feelings as adults, and they may show their emotions in different ways. Talk with your child about feelings and how feelings can be shown. Answer questions to the best of your ability, but if you don't know the answer, it's okay to say, "I don't know. What do you think?" Explore your family beliefs and knowledge with your child.

Family Activities

☒ Go for a walk with your child in a park, woods, or field and observe both living and dead things and how they depend on one another. Collect a dead insect in a cup or container and find a spot to have a burial or other ceremony with your child.

☒ Gather pictures of dead relatives and discuss with your child things you remember about them. If you attended funerals or ceremonies for the relatives, describe what took place.

Ideas Please

☒ Tell us about the death rituals your family follows.

Items Please

☒ We need shoeboxes, sympathy cards, seed packets and catalogues, and potting material.

# Children's Activities

Dead or Alive

Go on a classroom or playground safari to hunt for things that are dead or alive. Keep a list of things the children identify as dead and those identified as alive. After a list has been developed of approximately 3 to 5 things in each category, return to the large group. Use examples from each list and ask why children think each thing is either dead or alive and what makes them that way. As the children discuss this, the teacher can list the characteristics children use to determine when something is alive or dead.

Materials
clipboard, paper, large piece of newsprint or poster board, markers

Other Ideas

- Collect things that children think are in each category and discuss the items during group time.
- Show children several things from the classroom and ask if they think each is alive or dead.
- Play "Safari," by Eek-A-Mouse (*Reggae for Kids*. RAS, 3095).

What Happens When It Dies?

Have children gather leaves, twigs, or dead bugs from the ground and bring them into the classroom. Use gloves or a cup to scoop up dead bugs. Set up a special graveyard space in the classroom for the leaves, twigs, and bugs. Let each child or group be responsible for designing a marker or gravestone that describes the item, either with words or pictures. Let the children observe what happens over the course of time to each item in their graveyard. Their observations can be recorded using a book, chart, drawing, photograph, or video, with assistance from the teacher as needed.

Materials
newsprint, poster board, blank paper, markers, crayons, colored pencils, video camera and videotape (if desired), camera and film (if desired), graveyard (space covered by plastic, or an easily cleaned surface)

Other Ideas

- Place a vegetable or a piece of bread in a plastic bag or clear container and monitor what happens to it.
- Read *Remember the Butterflies*, by Anna Grossnickle Hines (New York: Dutton, 1991).
- Read *The Dead Bird*, by Margaret Wise Brown (New York: Harper, 1965).

Remembering the Good Things

This activity can be used at any time, but may be most useful when a child in the classroom experiences the death of a pet, relative, or someone they know, or in conjunction with other activities when children express personal loss. Set aside a special time within a couple of days of the loss and invite any child to bring photos or drawings of someone or something they knew that died. Encourage each child who brings a picture to share with friends throughout the day and to tell them something they really liked about the person, animal, or plant that died. During a special group time, ask any children who brought pictures to display them in a special spot set aside for the activity. Once the picture is displayed, ask the child who brought the picture or other children in the group to share something positive about the person, pet, or object. Record words used to describe the person. Encourage children who brought pictures to offer special "giggle stories" to the group (things about the person that made them laugh).

Materials

newsprint, markers, space to display photos or drawings

Other Ideas

- Children may want to create and sing a song about someone they knew who died.
- Invite children to sing the favorite song of a person who died.
- Read *The Wall*, by Eve Bunting (New York: Clarion, 1990).
- Play "The Letter," by Holly Near (*Sky Dances*. Redwood, 8902).

The Cemetery

Arrange for children to visit a graveyard or pet cemetery where a burial is about to take place or has recently taken place. Try to time the visit so that children can see the plot being dug or preparations being set up for a service. Ask children questions regarding how they think the grave is made, where they think people will sit, who might come to the funeral, and what happens at the funeral and afterward. Children may want to form groups to complete such projects as studying or drawing the different flowers on graves, making a flower arrangement for a grave, or measuring and recording the size of plots. Other projects include making rubbings of gravestones using clay, aluminum foil, or paper and markers (be sure to have children clean any rubbing areas first), or looking for the newest and oldest graves and, with help from the teacher, determining how long ago the person or pet was buried. Have small groups share their project results with the class.

Materials

tracing paper or thin newsprint, rolling pin, charcoal, markers, colored chalk, crayons, colored pencils, paper towels and water for cleaning discarded flower arrangements, dried flowers, plastic bottles (clean and empty), scissors, garbage bag and trash bag ties, masking tape, classroom space for cemetery display, aluminum foil, clay, thin metal plates

Other Ideas

- Role-play a burial for a doll.
- Take pictures of cemeteries or burial grounds and have children look at the pictures and discuss what they see.

Life and Death

Divide the children into groups to grow vegetables and flowers. Each group gathers information regarding when and how to grow what they have selected. If appropriate lighting is available, plants can be grown in the classroom. If room permits, plants can be grown outside during spring. Beginning with seeds or small plants, they watch the progress, report what they see to the large group, measure the growth, take pictures or make drawings of their plants at different stages, determine who is to care for the plant, discover if their plants have seeds and what they look like, and wait to see what happens when their plant dies. At each stage of plant development, ask the children if they can think of anything that happens to people that is similar to what happens to their plants.

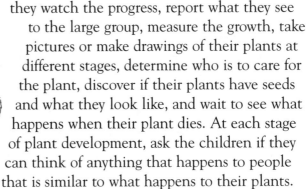

Materials

flower seeds, vegetable seeds, young plants, watering container, mulch, dirt, peat moss, measuring device (ruler, yardstick), camera and film (if desired), containers for seeds/plants, lighting for indoor plants (grow light, florescent light)

Other Ideas

- Visit a nearby farm, field, or park during different times of the year and take pictures or document on a chart what things are living, growing, or being planted or harvested.
- Visit a nursery and find out about the job of caring for plants.

My Family, My Community, My World

Children probably think of their family as the people who live under the same roof with them. Their primary parent or parents may be a father, mother, sibling, aunt, uncle, stepparent, foster parent, or other guardian. In addition, many children will have extended families and may have a home in more than one place. A child's sense of family, parent, home, and community, therefore, may be defined in a variety of ways.

Children develop a sense of security and self-worth by becoming familiar with themselves, their family, and the world around them. Helping children identify ways they can help out at home, school, and in their neighborhood will provide them with a feeling of accomplishment and belonging.

This theme will help children identify a variety of family types, examine their role in their family, learn ways they can help at home, begin to explore the world outside of their families, and learn about ways to improve their surroundings.

Addressing Diversity

Families, neighborhoods, and communities can vary greatly, and children generally only recognize the existence of family types and living arrangements similar to theirs or those around them. It is important to include many styles and types of families, living accommodations, and neighborhoods when introducing this theme. The definition of family should be broad and inclusive of every child's situation. Actively seek the participation of each family when presenting topics so that children will be exposed to a variety of cultures, languages, family structures, living accommodations, and roles that people perform in their family or community.

Where Will the Theme Lead?

Use these words to stimulate ideas for follow-up activities:

mother-in-law	stepsister	apartment	handicap	dwelling
grown-up	gay	census	accessible	den
generation	lesbian	herd	ecology	contribution
interracial	extended	nest	subdivision	landscape
sibling	divorce	earth	recycle	population
daddy	blended	trailer park	attic	community

Learning Center Materials

Dramatic Play:
framed pictures of families
photo album or magazine pictures of families
buckets, sponges, feather duster
large boxes to use for making a house or
  building
trash cans for role-playing
telephone book, maps, and keys
aprons, coveralls
empty, clean aluminum cans
brooms, mops, dust rags

Table Toys:
dollhouse and doll families
small buildings, homes
play fencing and landscape pieces
house, farm, city, and people puzzles
screws, screwdriver, and soft wood
craft sticks, twigs, moss
keys and locks
toilet paper tubes
community building sets

Language Arts:
stuffed animal family
home movies or videos
music about local towns,
  cities, or states
resource materials on your community
recordings of nature sounds
post cards, stationery, envelopes
wedding/birth announcements
home sale and/or rental ads
puppet families

Science:
family tree charts or pictures
maps, atlas, globe
aerial photos
containers to hold recyclables
plans for landscape, buildings,
  or homes
sample building supply materials
wood chips, mulch
water table with houseboats
door knobs to disassemble
can crusher and cans

Blocks:
paper dolls
wooden figures
boxes
bricks
wood chips
paper towel tubes
copy/fax paper tubes
pictures of land from landscaped
  homes and parks
scrap carpet pieces
paper cups

Art:
box lids to make frames
copies of children's family photos
plastic, silk, or dried flowers
pictures of landscapes and gardens
paint and wallpaper samples
shredded paper, confetti
twigs, mulch, straw, moss
small boxes
graph paper, scrap paper
Easter basket grass

Outside:
paintbrush with water
rakes
landscaping materials
trash bags
work gloves, hard hats, goggles
wagons, carts, dolly, wheelbarrow
straw or leaves
bricks
large cardboard pieces and tape
chalk to draw families and homes
wood tools to make frames

Library Books:
*My Mother's House, My Father's
  House,* by C.B. Christiansen
  (New York: Puffin, 1990).
Who's in a Family? by Robert Skutch (Berkeley,
  CA: Tricycle, 1995).
*Brother Eagle, Sister Sky, A Message from Chief
  Seattle* (New York: Dial, 1991).
The Earth and I, by Frank Asch (San Diego, CA:
  Gulliver, 1994).

Topic 1
Families

Learning Objectives:

☑ Children will identify members of their family.

☑ Children will identify words associated with families.

☑ Children will express curiosity and acceptance of different family structures.

Always keep family information confidential, whether it is shared by children in the classroom or provided by family members. Be sure to keep current records regarding emergency contacts for each child and any special help a child might need.

Avoid using phrases such as "take this home to your mother," since many children may be living with someone other than a mother. Use books, pictures, songs, and words that include references to many different grown-ups that might be responsible for children.

Actively seek participation by every child's family, since this is the best way to incorporate and include family structure, relationships, culture, community, and environmental concerns relevant to each child's situation. When children encounter family styles or family activities different from their own, encourage acceptance and use reassuring words and phrases so that children feel comfortable about their own family and other families.

Creating the Environment

The ideal environment would include books, pictures, and music representing every kind of family. Make the classroom a welcome place for the children's grown-ups by providing bulletin board displays, mail boxes, and lending libraries especially for adults. Solicit ideas from all families regarding classroom visitors, family events, field trips, and activities so that the interests of a variety of families will be represented.

Evaluation:

☒ Are children acting out different family roles during play?

☒ Do children talk about their families and ask about other families during conversation?

☒ Are children using vocabulary associated with families?

Family
Information
& Activity
Bulletin

Families

There are many different family structures, and each one is special in its own way. Young children first recognize their immediate family, the people they live with. Next, they may identify extended family, such as grandparents, aunts, or stepfamily members. Children need a sense of belonging and the security of a family, whether it is a single parent and one child, an aunt and several cousins, or two parents and many children.

Family structures sometimes change due to death, divorce, marriage, or the addition of a brother or sister. Discuss family changes and their impact with your child so that changes will be less confusing and frightening.

OUR FAMILIES

Family Activity

☒ Take a walk around the neighborhood with your child and observe different families. Discuss similarities and differences in the families and activities in which they are involved.

Ideas Please

☒ Tell us about your family and special activities, traditions, songs, and books.

Items Please

☒ Please send pictures of your family group or individual members. Photos will be photocopied for your child and then returned.

☒ Magazines, newspapers, junk mail, and catalogues depicting families or family activities would be very useful.

Children's Activities

Taking a Census

Talk about what a census is, how it is performed, and why it is performed. Involve each child in making a census booklet. Let them staple several pieces of blank paper together along with the instructions. (For safety reasons, have them place tape over the staples.) Include a copy of the instructions on the first sheet of the booklet. They will use the booklet to perform a census of their home, apartment, or living space.

Census Instructions

1) Draw a picture of everyone who lives in the same house, home, or apartment as you. If you live in more than one place, you can pick one place, or draw everyone in all places. You may include pets.

2) Work on your drawings at school and at home.

3) When you finish your drawings, you may share them during group time.

4) The teacher will label your drawings with the names of the people or pets.

5) When you finish telling us about your drawings, the teacher will help you count the people and pets and enter them on the census chart.

Materials

classroom census chart (include children's names and enough room to make marks for each family member), blank paper, instructions to attach to blank paper, markers, crayons, colored pencils, stapler, tape

Other Ideas

• Use family photographs attached to poster board to perform the census.

• Read *All Kinds of Families*, by Norma Simon (Morton Grove, IL: Whitman, 1976).

• Read *Asha's Mums*, by Rosamund Elwin and Michele Paulse (Toronto: Women's Press, 1990).

Family Slide Show

Ask children to bring in photographs and items that represent their families. Take slides of their photographs and items, getting as many close-ups as possible. Have the slides processed and then arrange them into a slide show, grouping each child's slides together. Assist each child in arranging their photos and items. Invite families to come and view the family slide show presentation. As each child's slides are shown, allow the child to provide narration regarding the pictures or items in each slide.

Materials

backdrops for family photographs, space for arranging items, slide film and camera, slide projector and screen, materials for children to create invitations, or teacher prepared invitations

Other Ideas

- Use a video camera to shoot a movie of each child's family photos and items. Present the "Family Movie" or "Family Slide Show" to other classrooms.
- Ask the children to pick a family member or pet and draw their picture, or make up a song about them and share their creations in large group.
- Read *The Lotus Seed*, by Sherry Garland (New York: Harcourt, 1993).
- Play "Free To Be...A Family," by The Melody Makers (*Free To Be...A Family*. A&M, 5196).

Puzzles, Puppets, and Playthings

Have children bring family photos, and make several photocopies of each, including enlargements of some. Establish a place for each child's copies and let them use the photocopies for the following activities: 1) Attach one photocopy to cardboard and cut into puzzle pieces. 2) Create a hand puppet by cutting out family members' faces and other body parts and attaching them with glue or tape to paper or an old sock. 3) Using Styrofoam, cardboard, or other free-standing material, assist children in attaching cutouts of family members to use as dollhouse figures or table toys. 4) Attach pictures of family members to cardboard and cut out to use as paper dolls.

Materials

Styrofoam, paper bags, old socks, photocopier, photocopies of family pictures, scissors, glue, tape, cardboard

Other Ideas

- Use photocopies of each child and family to mark their spaces, such as cubbies.

- Choose a family member's photo for each child and enlarge to make a mask.

- Let children choose a family picture cut from magazines to create stories or songs about the family.

- Involve children in using the copy machine to make their photocopies of family pictures.

- Play "Friendly Neighborhood," by Marlo Thomas (*Free To Be... A Family*. A&M, 5196).

Our Family Words

Ask children what they call their father, mother, sister, brother, grandfather, grandmother, aunt, uncle, and home. As you ask for other names for father (daddy, dad, pop) write each one down on a strip of paper. Put strips of paper in a hat or container. Then ask children to begin selecting names from the hat and, as each one is drawn, read it and ask them to decide what group or category it goes with.

Materials
marker, container, strips of paper

Other Ideas

- Extend this activity into the home by suggesting that children ask their grown-ups what terms they used for their mother, father, and other family members.

- Show a movie about a family and ask children, either separately or in groups, to make up stories or songs about what will happen next to the family from the movie.

- Read *My Two Uncles*, by Judith Vigna (Morton Grove, IL: Whitman, 1995).

- Read *Red Bird*, by Barbara Mitchell (New York: Lothrop, 1996).

Going, Going, Gone

Identify children who have moved from one place to another, from one home to another, or children who know someone who has moved to their building, town, or neighborhood. You can ask questions such as, "Have you ever moved to a new home?" or "Do you know anyone who has moved into your building or neighborhood?" Continue with such questions as, "If you have a new family in the neighborhood, how are they like your family?" "How is the new family different?" "What does a family do to get ready to move?" "What does a family have to pack?" "How does a family move their things?" "What is the nicest thing about moving to someplace new?" "How is a new place different?" "What does a family have to do after they move someplace new?" and "How do families make friends when they move?" For children who have recently moved into the area, ask questions like, "What kinds of families did you know where you used to live?" "How were they different from families here?" "How were they alike?" and "What did families do for fun where you used to live?" Allow children to ask questions about moving and explore ideas regarding families moving to a new place.

Materials
none needed

Other Ideas

- Provide boxes, suitcases, luggage carts, and a wagon for children to role-play moving or to use as props as they tell about moving.

- Visit a moving company.

- Read *Amelia's Road*, by Linda Jacobs Altman (New York: Lee, 1993).

Topic 2
I Help Others

Learning Objectives:

☑ Children will state ways each family member helps at home.

☑ Children will state ways they can help at home.

☑ Children will practice helping behaviors in the classroom.

☑ Children will identify many ways people can help.

Although there are individual differences, many children like to do things for themselves because it makes them feel good. Children may enjoy helping others if it is proposed in a positive way and the task is not too overwhelming. Some children may find it difficult to accept help from others and may see the help provided to them as taking away their freedom or power.

Children can help at home as they learn to take care of their dressing needs for the bathroom and prepare for outside play. At school, it may be necessary for children to develop independence skills due to the staff ratio and curriculum goals; however, respect should be shown for families whose practices encourage less independence. Children can be encouraged to help one another solve problems or clean up toys. They can also help one another feel better through kind words, playing together, and making gifts for one another. Chores in the classroom can be shared to reinforce helping.

Children are familiar with the roles each of their family members play and may be confused when they discover that things are different in other families. Encourage children to share with the class how their family members help one another at home. This allows children to explore similarities and differences in roles and identify the variety of ways people help one another. Books reflecting nonsexist roles for family members and a variety of helping behaviors may help children begin to see and accept differences.

Creating the Environment

The teacher can support children as they learn about helping by designing an environment that encourages children to act independently when selecting toys and returning them. Easily accessible, low shelves promote children returning materials and toys to their appropriate place. Children enjoy using props to role-play cleaning in dramatic play and making things for people with materials in the woodworking and art areas. Encourage children to prepare thank-you notes when people help them by providing paper in the language arts center. Incorporating pets and plants into the classroom and allowing children to assist with their care gives them an opportunity to practice helping behaviors.

Evaluation:

☒ Do children talk about ways their family members help at home?

☒ Do children show helping behaviors during role-playing?

☒ Are children participating in helping activities at school?

Family Information & Activity Bulletin

I Help at Home

Children like to do things they see their parents do. They can watch and learn to help with simple chores, such as folding clothes or setting the table. These can be fun activities that help your child develop skills. Please have lots of patience as your child learns to help. Children's work will not be complete or perfect. Your child may lose interest in an activity after just a few minutes, so try to break chores into smaller or shorter activities that allow for success and frequent stops and starts.

Each time your child tries to help, use praising words like, "I like it when you help" and "You did a good job." This builds confidence and helps your child feel good.

Family Activities

☒ Gather writing materials and sit down with your child. Together you can create a list of things your child can do to help around the house.

☒ Encourage your child to assist with putting away pots and pans, taking care of pets, matching socks, planting or weeding flowers, washing the car, dusting, mopping, raking leaves, painting a fence or room, cleaning up the yard, watering plants, or assembling shelves or furniture.

Ideas Please

☒ Please share with us your ideas about things children can do to help at home.

Items Please

☒ We would appreciate pictures of people helping, pictures of things that need maintenance or repairing, rags to use as dust cloths or for cleaning, and cleaned and empty plastic containers.

Children's Activities

Helping on the Inside

Prepare charts for a variety of areas that might be found in children's living spaces. Label each chart with a heading, such as "bedroom," "bathroom," "kitchen," "closet," "laundry," "garage," "basement," "attic," "living room." As you introduce this activity, realize that all children may not have a bedroom or typical living space, and reassure children that it's okay if their living space is different.

Ask children to think about and give examples of things they might find in each of the areas listed on the charts. Listen carefully to the examples children give and list them on the appropriate chart. When charts are complete, refer back to the things listed on each and ask children how they could help take care of each thing.

Materials

newsprint or poster board, markers

Other Ideas

- Let children come up with the categories for the charts.

- Help children develop a chart to take home for keeping track of ways they can help.

- Invite a sibling to come in and describe a chore they do at home.

- Read *Feast for 10*, by Cathryn Falwell (New York: Clarion, 1993).

- Play "Something for Everyone" by Marlo Thomas, Kermit the Frog, and the Muppets (*Free To Be...A Family*. A&M, 5196).

Helping Outside

Ask children to think about and give examples of things they might find outside their living space, like an apartment court, front gate, back yard, alley, driveway, or street. Help children understand that some people have yards and others may not.

Listen carefully and make a list as children give examples of what can be found in these places. Make a chart with the items listed for each outside place. Using the chart, ask children how they could help take care of the things listed.

Materials
newsprint or poster board, blank paper, markers

Other Ideas
- Help the children develop a chart to take home and use in tracking things they can help with.
- Invite a sibling to come in and describe a chore they do outside the living space.
- Read *My Steps*, by Sally Derby (New York: Lee, 1996).

Who Does It?

In a group, let children generate a list of jobs people do at home. Ask children to tell who in their home does each job. Add the person mentioned beside the items or jobs on the list, or have various possibilities listed across the top (daddy, mom, dad's partner, mom's partner, stepmother, stepfather, uncle, aunt, auntie, grandmother, gramps, sister, brother, cousin, or any other person represented in children's families). Put a check under the person's name when a child mentions that this person does a particular job at their house.

Materials
newsprint or poster board, markers

Other Ideas
- Discuss how people in different families have different roles.
- Invite a professional house cleaner or "fix-it" person to come into the classroom and tell about how they take care of families.
- Invite family members to talk about roles in their family. Include a variety of families.
- Read *My Daddy and I*, by Eloise Greenfield (New York: Black Butterfly, 1991).
- Read *When the Teddy Bears Came*, by Martin Waddell (Cambridge, MA: Candlewick, 1994).

How Do You Use It?

Gather several items used for cleaning or maintaining the home or living space. Assist small groups of children in disassembling and assembling various parts to these items. Show children how to install new bags and filters on vacuums, how to change sponges on mops, how to add string to the weed trimmer, how to empty the hand vacuum, how to change batteries in flashlights, and how to change the faucet aerator.

Materials

vacuums, vacuum bags and filters, weed trimmers and string, sponge mops and sponges, rags, flashlights and batteries, faucet and aerator, hand tools necessary for disassembling these items (screwdrivers, wrenches)

Other Ideas

- Visit a laundry and demonstrate to small groups the various knobs and parts of the washing machines and dryers. Show children where the water hoses and lint traps are, and explain how to clean components to increase the life of the machines.

- Provide old clocks, lamps, and other materials children can disassemble using tools.

- Visit a repair shop and observe the activity.

Handy Helpers

Explain to children that they are going to make a "Handy Helper" box and fill it with "Handy Helper" items. Have each child choose a box and use markers, glitter, and art supplies to add interesting touches to their boxes. Assist each child to attach string handles, cut handholds, or design a lid for their box or container. Add the child's name to their box, or let them copy or trace their names onto their boxes. Next, allow each child to select a rag or sock for cleaning or dusting and add it to their box. In addition, each child may choose an empty spray bottle, sponge, paper bag, toothbrush, and plastic scrubber to go in their boxes.

Materials

shoebox-sized boxes, clean rags, sponges, yarn, string, spray bottles (clean and empty), cloth, paper bags, toothbrushes, plastic scrubbers

Other Ideas

- Visit a hardware store or a variety store to see the different types of cleaning supplies and tools for helping around the house.

- Invite the school custodian to come in and share cleaning tips with children.

- Read *Tools*, by Ann Morris (New York: Lothrop, 1992).

Topic 3
My Community

Learning Objectives:

- ☑ Children will identify the name of their community.
- ☑ Children will identify other people who live near them.
- ☑ Children will state that people and animals live in different kinds of living spaces and communities.

Learning one's name, address, and telephone number is essential for a child's safety. The teacher should have the child's correct address and assist children in learning their addresses. Memorizing this information may be difficult for many children because the numbers appear to be meaningless and may be forgotten easily. Begin with the name of the community and help them build a sense of identity and belonging. Teachers may need to phrase questions in different ways for individual children. For example, a child may not understand the question "What is your address?" but may know "Where do you live?"

Discussions to identify other people who live near them may take place either individually or in small groups. It is helpful to allow time for questions and discussion so children can share information regarding different living spaces, homes, neighborhoods and communities they identify in their area, or that they are learning about. In this way children help other children see a wider range of possibilities for community structure.

Creating the Environment

The ideal environment would include pictures and materials that represent the communities children live in. Also helpful are materials that help identify addresses, such as phone books, mailing envelopes or labels, street address signs, and street maps.

Invite parents in community-helping roles to come into the classroom and describe their contributions. Ask parents in various community roles to give the children tours of where they work. Any parents who have lived in other communities, towns, states, or countries would make excellent guests in the classroom to talk about similarities and differences in housing, family environments, school environments, and community environments.

Use community resources, such as the chamber of commerce and tourist information bureaus, for materials to add to learning centers. Go for walks and take pictures or videos of the community and special events to infuse a community atmosphere into the classroom.

Evaluation:

☒ Are children talking about their community?

☒ Can children recite their address?

☒ Are children showing an interest in and acceptance of the differences in homes?

Family Information & Activity

....

Bulletin

My Community

Young children need to know their name, address, and phone number. When learning the address and phone number, it may be easier for your child if they sing or chant it. Practice saying, singing, or chanting the information in the car, at bedtime, or during meals.

Talk to your child about who you trust to take care of them, to pick them up from school, to take them someplace, or to help them in emergencies. Be sure your child knows the names of these people or how to identify people who can help, and the information they should give out.

Family Activities

☒ Walk with your child to a nearby location and read street signs, store signs, building names, and addresses on the way. Let the child be the leader on the way home and encourage them to identify from memory the streets, buildings, and stores along the way.

☒ Walk with your child to a significant spot, such as a playground, school, or neighbor's house. When you return home, assist them in drawing a map to guide them home using pictures and lines. You may have to make the journey several times before the map is complete.

Ideas Please

☒ Give us the names and addresses of relatives or friends so we can look for the locations on a map.

Items Please

☒ Please send us sale or rent advertisements, construction "how-to" brochures, old maps, keys, and architectural and home magazines.

Children's Activities

Home Show

Have children draw or bring in a picture of where they live. Some children may have more than one home and should be allowed to bring in or draw more than one picture. Help children fold poster board in half so it will stand up, and assist each child in attaching the pictures or drawings to the top in a way that will not destroy them when removed. Add each child's name. When asking for pictures of living space, be sure that parents understand that the picture the child brings to the classroom will be displayed.

Materials

poster board, markers, tape, string, clothespins, fasteners for attaching pictures (photo corner fasteners, envelope corners)

Other Ideas

- Display the poster boards around the room and allow children to invite other children to view their picture or drawing while they tell them things they like best about where they live.

- Go on a field trip to see many kinds of homes, including some of the children's homes.

- Read *This is Our House,* by Michael Rosen (Cambridge, MA: Candlewick, 1996).

Where Do Other People and Things Live?

Ask children to look through old magazines and newspapers and cut out as many different pictures as they can find of houses or places where people or animals live. Help children locate and use some magazines that might include housing that is different.

Once the children have cut out and collected pictures of houses and living spaces, have them attach the pictures to cardboard or another solid material that will allow the pictures to stand upright. Encourage children to make displays of various environments, such as homes, yards, neighborhoods, and cities, using plastic figures and the pictures of items that they have collected and assembled.

Materials

scissors, cardboard, glue or tape, small plastic figures, magazines (architectural, travel, pet, nature)

Other Ideas

- Once displays have been completed by the children, "visit" each with the large group and ask the children questions such as, "If you lived here, would this area or space belong just to you?" "Would you need to share this space with your family?" "Would you need to share this space with anyone else? With friends, neighbors, plants, trees, animals?" "Who takes care of this space?" "Can you do anything to make this space nicer?"

- During group time, visit the displays one at a time and ask the children to describe them. Record their descriptive words on poster board or paper and place them below the displays.

- Have the children look for places where animals live, including birds and insects, and make posters.

- Use magazine pictures to make a scrapbook, collage, or bulletin board display.

House Construction

Engage children in a conversation about their living space and have them describe many things about it. Provide blocks for children and have them build a place similar to their living space. Help each child write their address to put in front of their structure. Take pictures of each child's living space to include in their book about their home and community.

Materials
blocks, camera, film, paper, marker, art supplies, children's addresses

Other Ideas

- Provide wood and tools and encourage children to build a miniature house.

- Visit a store to see birdhouses, doghouses, and other pet homes.

- Provide many keys for sorting, tracing, stringing, and trying in locks.

- Read *Houses and Homes,* by Ann Morris (New York: Lothrop, 1992).

- Read *Priscilla Twice,* by Judith Caseley (New York: Greenwillow, 1995).

- Listen to "We Love Our Home" by Francine Lancaster (*Peace Is The World Smiling.* Music for Little People, 2104).

Where Am I?

In group discussions, ask children what country, state, and city they live in. Show them where their state, city, or town is located on a map or globe. On a map that can remain displayed, highlight or outline the state you live in. Use a round sticker to indicate the location of your city or town. If children come from other towns or suburbs, use additional stickers to designate approximately where those places are. Make large labels with the names of the state, cities, and towns where the children live, and place those on the map close to the appropriate stickers. Locate states or cities where children's relatives live too.

Materials

maps, globes, markers, labels, stickers, relatives' addresses, children's addresses

Other Ideas

- While displaying a map or drawing of your state, ask the children to make a shape like the state with modeling clay or to draw a picture of the state. Before the clay dries, children may want to make a small hole near the top so that their artwork can be hung up.

- Invite a mail carrier to visit and explain why addresses are important.

- Provide stationery, envelopes, and stamps for children to write and send a letter to themselves or a relative.

- Read *Going Home*, by Eve Bunting (New York: Harper, 1996).

- Play "This Old Man," by Yellowman (*Reggae For Kids*. RAS, 3095).

Current Events

Discuss things that happen in the neighborhood, town, city, and state. Clip articles and pictures from newspapers, record a radio news story, or videotape a television news story that involves area events and topics in which the children might be interested. School ball games, events siblings are in, and celebrations may be of interest. Ask children to bring in recent copies of newspapers from home, if they would like. During group time, share information from a variety of articles or sources that you have, and from newspaper articles that children bring. Always emphasize the name of the town, place, or state where the event took place so that children become familiar with the use of the names of their neighborhood, city, town, and state. Refer to any maps or pictures of places that are displayed in the room or in the article when sharing the information.

Materials

newspapers, radio, television, videotape recorder (if desired), tape recorder (if desired), video and audio tape players

Other Ideas

- Ask children if they want to tell the group about anything exciting that happened in their neighborhood, building, city, or town. Encourage the child telling about an event to give exact names of places involved.
- Use the paper to identify events to attend on field trips.
- Invite individuals from the media to come and tell about the stories they have covered.

Topic 4
I Help My Environment

Learning Objectives:

☑ Children will identify various environments (classroom, playground, street, home).

☑ Children will pick up trash and put away toys and tools.

☑ Children will state ways we can help the environment.

☑ Children will begin to see that they are part of a larger world.

An environment is a surrounding area. Since people are very mobile, children move in and out of many different environments. They will not completely understand or be able to define the term *environment*. With appropriate use and learning activities, however, children should be able to recognize different environments or areas with which they are familiar. Examples of their environments include the classroom, the playground, their home, and the street on which they live.

Young children cannot comprehend an environment beyond that which they can see. While older children can recognize that their home is part of a larger community, younger children can only relate to their own home and other homes they see around them.

Young children learn through concrete experiences. A child who has never seen a pond, lake, river, or ocean cannot comprehend a large area of water with fish and other living creatures. Therefore, it is not appropriate to talk about water pollution as a global idea and expect children to comprehend. If there is a body of water in your area, children can understand keeping that environment clean since they can actually see it.

Many of the activities listed in this section require children to carry out tasks at home or bring in something from home. Make parents aware of projects the children may choose to work on well in advance so that they can help find needed items or be available to assist the child in carrying out their project. Send home lists of common household things that might be recycled into classroom materials if parents are willing to save and send in the items.

Creating the Environment

The ideal environment would include opportunities to practice caring for the various environments with which children come in contact. Modeling of conservation, recycling, reusing, and beautification helps children attach concrete actions to these concepts. Teacher modeling may include showing children how to use water wisely, reusing or recycling materials from home for various learning centers, collecting other materials to take to recycling centers, and adding plants and pictures to the classroom. A fish tank in the classroom can help children who do not live close to any body of water learn about keeping water clean. Assisting with the care and cleaning of space for a classroom pet is another way children see how environments impact living things.

Evaluation:

☒ Are children talking about their environment?

☒ Are children participating in environmental education activities?

☒ Does role-play activity relate to taking care of the environment?

Family Information & Activity

Bulletin

I Help My Environment

As children begin to recognize which bedroom, house, classroom, or playground is theirs, work with them to learn to take care of their toys, pets, or other items in the home environment. Talk with them about how we are taking care of our environment when we put our toys away after use and when we put trash in the trash can.

As children grow older, they will learn that their home and school environment is part of a larger environment, such as a neighborhood or community. Talk about ways to care for these environments, such as recycling, planting flowers and trees, and putting trash where it belongs.

Family Activities

☒ With help from your child, plant a tree in the backyard, add live flowers to a room or garden, or clean some part of the home.

☒ Set up recycling containers, bins, boxes, or bags with help and information supplied by your child.

☒ Review the "In My World" drawings with your child. Help your child identify and draw additional items and return the pictures the next day.

☒ Pick a day to clean a street, building, or neighborhood with your child.

Ideas Please

☒ Give us ideas about songs to use to teach children about the environment.

☒ Give us ideas for projects to improve the environment or community.

Items Please

☒ We could use things like scrap paper, lids, empty fruit baskets, net bags, broken jewelry, boxes, bags, empty toilet paper or paper towel tubes.

Children's Activities

In My World

Ask children to draw pictures or make clay representations of something in their bedrooms or sleeping spaces. After displaying their completed work to the group, ask them to tell about it. As each thing is named, ask how they take care of that item ("How do you take care of your bed?" "How do you take care of your clothes?" "How do you take care of your stuffed animal?").

Materials
drawing paper, markers, paint, colored pencils, crayons, clay

Other Ideas

- Ask children to draw pictures of things outside their home or living space. Ask the same type of questions ("How do you take care of...") regarding such things as trees, cars, plants, animals, buildings, sidewalks, and grass.

- Have children trace an object from school and then make a mosaic by gluing small pieces of cut paper inside the picture. Discuss with children how to care for each object they traced.

- Have children pick an object in the classroom or at home and make up a poem or story about it. After each child shares their poem or story, discuss the care of the object.

Respect My Space

Have each child pick an item from their own room or outside that they are going to be responsible for, care for, clean, or organize. Tape record children telling their plan for caring for, cleaning, or organizing the item. After they have carried out their plan, have children report.

Materials
tape recorder, blank tape

Other Ideas

- Have groups or individuals take care of different things in the classroom.

- Take the class to volunteer at a nursing home and help put away supplies after an activity.

- Arrange for the class to donate artwork for a display at a bank. Children should take special care of work to be donated.
- Read *City Green*, by DyAnne DiSalvo-Ryan (New York: Morrow, 1994).
- Play "Turn The World Around," by Music for Little People Kids Choir (*Peace Is The World Smiling*. Music for Little People, 2104).

Don't Waste It, Dump It, or Pollute It

Visit a recycling center, a sanitary landfill or dump, or nearby body of water. Prepare the children for the visit by reading stories that contain references to these places. Assist the children in accessing additional reference materials. Look at pictures of these types of places and have a "share what you know" group time where children ask questions and other children volunteer information regarding the topic.

Materials
stories and reference materials that include information about landfills, recycling centers, and pollution

Other Ideas
- During the trips, ask children to identify items they see that have been sent to be recycled at the recycling center, that have been dumped at the landfill, and that have been thrown into the water.
- During group time, ask children to name items from each place visited, with the teacher making a list of items mentioned from each place.
- Invite people who work at a recycling center or landfill to visit and talk about their jobs.
- Help children write letters to environmental groups to request information.
- Ask older siblings to tell about recycling projects they know about.
- Read *Where Once There Was a Wood*, by Denise Fleming (New York: Holt, 1996).
- Play "On My Pond," by Kermit the Frog and the Muppets (*Free To Be...A Family*. A&M, 5196).

Stash the Trash

After studying about recycling, ask children to suggest items that can be recycled or reused. Make a list of their suggestions, and ask which items might be found in the classroom. Choose a trash container least likely to present health risks and perform an examination of current classroom trash. Demonstrate proper trash handling by wearing gloves, glasses, and an apron, and by washing hands after handling any trash. Let children put on gloves and goggles or glasses and examine the trash in the selected container. As each item is handled, ask whether it could be recycled or reused. Add the items that children suggest to the list of recyclables and reusables. Decide which items to reuse in learning centers and which to take to a recycling center.

Ask the children for ideas about how to sort and classify materials to be recycled. Allow children to create a recycling plan and help them think of supplies needed to carry it out. Let the children put their plan into action. Help them find the needed supplies to prevent spilling and to label bags, boxes, and containers. Help children determine where to take items for disposal. Remind children to wash their hands after handling any trash and to wear protective gloves and clothing when sorting trash.

Materials
boxes and bags, bag ties, tape, markers, blank paper, newsprint, gloves, goggles, aprons, other protective clothing, wagon or rolling cart, water for cleaning up

Other Ideas
• Play "Conviction of the Heart," by Kenny Loggins (*Leap of Faith*. Columbia, 46140).

Teaching Others

After children have visited a recycling center or studied about recycling, have them discuss things they would say to people to teach them how to recycle. During the discussion, take careful notes regarding their ideas. Ask them to role-play their ideas. After they have practiced and role-played, videotape the children teaching about recycling. Have the children watch the videotape and be willing to reshoot or make another tape if they would like to improve on their technique. The final version can be introduced to other classes, shown at open house or community events, or sent to a local television station.

Materials
video camera, videotape player, props and costumes, markers, newsprint, pictures or signs about the topic

Other Ideas
• Children can divide into groups and role-play teaching different environmental concepts they have learned about, such as "don't pollute," "don't waste," "clean up your mess," "recycle and reuse," "dumping is dirty," or "take care of your space." Allow children to help videotape and direct one another's groups. In this way several videotapes can be produced.
• Play and sing "Garbage Blues," by Tickle Tune Typhoon (*Hug The Earth*. Tickle Tune Typhoon Records).

Chapter 6

Be Safe,
Not Sorry

Safety education is essential to help children develop awareness for a safer life. It involves teaching children safe actions as well as helping them understand possible consequences for unsafe behavior. Help children realize that they can control some aspects of their safety through certain actions. Teach safety in a way that does not frighten children but helps them see the importance of taking care of themselves.

This theme will introduce the child to lifelong habits that promote safety. Introduction to safety habits in daily living outside the school environment will also occur. Children will gain a higher measure of confidence as they learn about safety and begin to incorporate actions into their lives that make them feel more safe.

Topics presented include use of seat belts, pedestrian safety, weapons avoidance, and fire/burn prevention. These topics were selected because of the high rate of child injury and death related to them. Other safety topics are presented throughout this curriculum and integrated within themes, as appropriate.

Addressing Diversity

Individualizing this theme for the children in your class and the community is necessary. Safety activities and rules should be based upon the greatest hazards, threats, and needs in your community. Remember that safety rules and supervision may differ at home. Do not judge differences, since parents know better their child's needs and abilities in that environment.

Where Will the Theme Lead?

Use these words to stimulate ideas for follow-up activities:

laws	sprinklers	prison	war	harness
hazards	temperature	fireworks	insulation	valve
vehicle	reflective	Fahrenheit	solar panels	absorb
peace	clothing	rickshaw	crosswalk	accident
education	axle	distance	gang	helmet
hunting	wreck	flammable	fireplace	knee pads

Learning Center Materials

Dramatic Play:
belts and belt hanger
luggage cart and tie-down
shoes that buckle
reflective clothing
flashlights
cellophane paper (red, yellow, green)
candles and holders
empty fire extinguisher without pin
baby stroller

Table Toys:
game and instructions
homemade puzzle that states rules
transportation puzzles
lacing
homemade puzzle depicting weapons
building sets with wheels
playhouse vehicles and traffic signs
traffic puzzles and games
clips, hooks, and other fasteners

Language Arts:
sample rules and safety signs
sample speeding and parking tickets
appliance instructions and warranties
new car brochures
hunting magazines
smoke detector in box with directions
rebus directions for any activity
brochures about solar heating

Science:
photographs of caution signs
sewing hooks and eyes
luggage straps with belt hooks
small tires and wheels
reflectors
spools and dowel rods
  to create axles
cars to take apart
smoke detector to take apart
ashes from fireplace
fireplace shovel

Blocks:
safety signs for props
string, rope, leather lacing, and yarn
belt buckles for hauling
vehicles (bus, train, truck, planes)
traffic signs
small exit signs
pictures of buildings on fire
fire truck
car garages

Art:
tools that require caution
  (stapler, scissors, tools
  to work with clay)
old belts to cut and glue
small cars to roll through paint
string, yarn, rope pieces
wood squares to sand and paint signs on
tissue paper (red, gray, orange, yellow,
  and blue)
clay and pictures of candleholders

Outside:
street maps
air pump and tires to fill
old tricycle and tools
reflectors
horns
paper and pencils to issue
  "speeding tickets"
sections of garden hose
thermometer

Library Books:
Colors Everywhere, by Tana
  Hoban (New York:
  Greenwillow, 1994).
Mama Zooms, by Jane Cowen (New York:
  Scholastic, 1993).
Tikvah Means Hope, by Patricia Polacco (New
  York: Doubleday, 1994).

144

Topic 1
My Safety Rules

Learning Objectives:

☑ Children will state safety rules for classroom, playground, and/or bus.

☑ Children will practice safety rules in classroom, playground, and/or bus.

☑ Children will explain why rules are different in different places.

☑ Children will identify reasons for rules.

Integration of safety awareness with appropriate behavior reinforces learning and helps children feel successful. The purpose of safety rules or guidance, however, is to promote awareness and to encourage developmentally appropriate behavior that prevents injury. This guidance is most effective when staff have appropriate expectations and safety rules are stated in a positive manner. For example, an indoor safety rule might relate to walking versus running. An appropriate safety rule might be stated "We walk indoors," rather than the negative "Do not run indoors." This positive statement reflects and reinforces the child's daily appropriate behavior, whereas the negative statement implies correction of an inappropriate behavior.

Limit the number of rules or guidelines. When a teacher creates a rule for every activity, it results in a long list. Children and staff may become frustrated when they can't remember all the rules, which may result in some essential safety rules being overlooked. Children cannot be expected to remember all of the specific rules. Gently remind children as needed. With positive reinforcement, children will begin to follow safety rules with increasing consistency. As children develop greater understanding of safety rules, they begin to develop self-control and feel more secure.

Creating the Environment

Create a safe and inviting environment for children. When the environment is free of potential hazards, staff spend less time saying "no" and more time in positive interaction with the children. Furthermore, if children are allowed to explore without risk of injury, they develop a sense of security and confidence.

.Carefully inspect both the indoor and outdoor environment and modify them as needed for safety. Consider the following:

- Firmly secure furniture and equipment to prevent falling (bolt tall bookshelves to the wall, anchor playground equipment).
- Check for sharp corners and edges, protrusions (nails or screws sticking out), pinch points, and entrapment areas ($3^{1}/2$ to 9 inch openings).
- Keep materials and equipment clean and in good working order.
- Playground equipment size, location, construction, installation, surfacing, and maintenance are all factors that contribute to safety. Contact the Consumer Product Safety Commission (800-638-2772) for additional information.
- Adults and children may find it helpful to have safety rules posted as reminders.

Evaluation:

☒ Are children talking about different rules?

☒ Do children practice following the rules at school?

☒ During dramatic play, are children making, following, and enforcing rules?

Family Information & Activity Bulletin

My Safety Rules

Young children may be able to state safety rules, but may not remember, understand, or know how to obey them. Decide on two or three of the most important safety rules for your child. If you live in a city, an essential rule may be "stay in the yard" (away from the street). In rural areas, a basic rule might be "stay away from the pond unless an adult is with you." It may help a child remember the rules if you also discuss why you have each rule. For example, "If you leave the yard and go in the street, a car might hit you and hurt you." It's important for children to be aware of safety and understand the rules. It's even more important for adults to make the environment as safe as possible, and to supervise children.

Family Activity

☒ Take a walk or go for a drive with your child and look for safety rules. Read the rules to your child. Talk about what the rules mean, why they exist, and if you agree with them.

Ideas Please

☒ Let us know about places your family goes where rules are posted.

☒ Tell us about your family rules.

Items Please

☒ Send us copies of any written rules from businesses, schools, or recreation facilities.

☒ Send pictures of people doing things that may be dangerous if there were no rules.

# Children's Activities

The Rule Book

Before this activity, write the title "Rule Book" on the first page of a chart tablet and involve a few children in illustrating this page. Write in small print "Illustrated By" and the children's names who contributed.

Gather children and tell them you want them to help you write a book about rules. Say that you will meet several times to work on it. Introduce the illustrators of the title page and assure children that everyone will get to contribute. Explain that you will ask them some questions and will write down what they say so it can be read later.

On the next page, write "What We Know About Rules" and tell children what it says. Ask what they think you should write there. Listen and encourage children to talk. Tell children that the next time you meet, you will ask for examples of rules, so they might want to ask their family members for some ideas. After children have shared, thank them and ask if there is a volunteer to work on illustrating the completed section. Follow by supporting and crediting the illustrators.

During future meetings, ask children to work on each of these topics: What are some rules? Why do we have rules? and How can we find out more about rules? Also add topics to the book that are of local interest.

Materials
24 by 16 inch tablet, marker, art supplies

Other Ideas
- Encourage each child to make a rule book on chart paper.
- Read *Officer Buckle and Gloria*, by Peggy Rathmann (New York: Putnam, 1995).

The Rule Hunt

Arrange to visit places to see posted rules and talk to experts. Locations to visit could include other classrooms, playgrounds, restaurants, skating rinks, swimming pools, theaters, schools, pet stores, airports, or other public places.

Announce that you are going to look for rules and interview people who make up rules or enforce them. Explain about enforcement. Help children decide which questions to ask. When posted rules are spotted on the trip, see if children can predict what the rules say. Read all rules aloud and take a picture of them. Encourage children to ask questions of the experts who work at the site where rules are spotted. Keep notes and photograph the children as they look at rules and interview people. Help children ask people who do not work at the site what they think about the rules. Assist children in designing and sending thank-you notes to each place visited.

Materials
camera, film, paper, pen, art supplies

Other Ideas

• Visit elected officials to ask about local community rules.

• Visit or invite a state legislator to talk about rules and laws.

• Invite a lifeguard to tell about water rules.

The Rule Hunt Report

Before this activity, get the pictures developed and review notes from the field trip (see previous activity). Write "The Rule Hunt Report" at the top of poster board and read this aloud to children. Prompt children to think about the rules they saw and the experts they interviewed. Refer to your notes and give children needed information. Encourage them to tell what they remember so you can write it down. Show them the pictures and see if there are more comments. Ask if they have information about what people who did not work there thought of the rules. Ask children what they thought of the rules at each place. Invite ideas from the children and adults in the room. Contribute ideas you have too. Ask for volunteers to illustrate, attach pictures, and make the poster board into a book. Place the book where children can access and view it.

Materials
poster board, marker, pictures of rules, notes of the visits, art supplies

Other Ideas

• Use the pictures from the trip to make puzzles.

• Make a video of the children's report and send copies to the managers of the places visited.

Home Rules

Write "Home Rules" at the top of construction paper and read it aloud to children. Ask children to share rules from home while you write what they say using a different piece of construction paper for each child. Solicit input from children and adults in the room. Ask if they think the rules should be the same at home and at school. Let children illustrate their own sheets, and then post the sheets in a display area.

Materials
construction paper, marker, art supplies

Other Ideas

- Invite parents and older siblings to visit and tell about family rules.
- Read *No Jumping on the Bed,* by Ted Arnold (New York: Dial, 1987).

School Safety Rules

Write "Classroom and Playground Safety Rules" at the top of a white board and read it aloud to the children. See if anyone has ideas about what the rules should be. Solicit input from children and adults in the room. Encourage them to look around the room and to think of the activities that happen every day. Take children to the playground to look around and think about what happens there. As ideas for rules are stated, write them down and ask children to help decide if each rule should be used. Modify them if the group thinks there should be changes. Ask for volunteer illustrators. Give them any needed support, and credit them for their work.

Materials
white board, markers

Other Ideas

- Visit other classrooms to discover what their rules are.
- Invite a teacher or children from another class to show and tell their class rules.
- Help children develop safety rules for the bus.
- Let each child make a bus out of a shoebox. Give them a copy of school bus rules to glue to their bus.

Topic 2
Green, Yellow, Red

Learning Objectives:

☑ Children will identify traffic personnel.

☑ Children will demonstrate "stop, look, listen" before crossing the street.

☑ Children will state that traffic signs and signals are for safety.

Incidents involving moving vehicles are a leading cause of injury and death for young children. Several factors put young children at risk. First, drivers may not see a small child who is playing in the street, on a tricycle, or between parked cars. The second factor involves the misconception of many young children who believe that if they can see the car, the driver of the car can see them.

Children's sensory development is another factor. Children under age six cannot accurately determine if a vehicle is coming toward or going away from them, the distance of the vehicle, or the speed. A young child can say "stop, look, and listen," but may misjudge and cross in front of an oncoming vehicle.

Children are impulsive in their actions. If a ball rolls into the street, a child is very likely to run after it. When teaching children about traffic safety, stress that they can get another ball, but they cannot get another body. Teachers must be aware of the potential risks when children are on field trips, entering or exiting a bus or other vehicle, on nature walks near a street, or on unfenced playgrounds.

Consider the community and environment when teaching traffic safety. In rural areas, the greatest dangers may be home driveways, avoiding farm equipment, or crossing a road to the mailbox. In small communities and neighborhoods, children often play on sidewalks or driveways and may learn to cross streets to play with neighboring children. In urban areas, children may live or play near high traffic areas that may or may not have pedestrian crossings and traffic signals.

Creating the Environment

Indoor and outdoor play areas can be used to simulate traffic and pedestrian areas. Check your community for types of traffic signals, signs, and safety personnel, and include props such as traffic signs and crossing guard vests in the classroom. Designate "streets and roads" on the playground or tricycle paths so children can practice both pedestrian and vehicle safety awareness. Set up a learning center in a large area to represent a street or road crossing, or create a table game with streets, vehicles, and figures of people. As children play, teachers can encourage them to talk about or clearly show what they are doing ("stop, look, and listen").

For child safety, make helmets available for all wheeled vehicles. Additionally, a fenced playground helps protect children from outside traffic.

Evaluation:

☒ During play, are children pretending to be traffic safety helpers?

☒ Are children becoming more aware of traffic and safety?

☒ Are children talking about traffic safety?

Family Information & Activity

Bulletin

Green, Yellow, Red

Moving vehicles can be one of the greatest dangers for children. Children may be injured while crossing a street, getting off the school bus, or while playing in their own driveway.

Children are impulsive. If their ball rolls into the street, they may run after it. Also, children under age six do not have the sensory development to judge if a vehicle is coming toward or going away from them, the distance of the vehicle, or the speed. A child may say "stop, look, and listen," but still cross in front of an oncoming

vehicle. Young children may also believe that if they can see the car, then the driver of the car can see them.

Vehicle drivers may not see a child playing in the street, on a tricycle or small bicycle, or between parked cars. Always check around your own vehicle before moving from your driveway. Talk to your child about the importance of your "outside" rules. A safety rule for your child might be "Streets, parking lots, and driveways are for cars. Backyards are for children."

Family Activities

☒ Go for a drive or walk to look for traffic signs and lights. Talk about what they mean.

☒ Talk to your child about the family rules regarding traffic safety.

Ideas Please

☒ Give us your ideas for field trips and guest speakers that would help your child learn about traffic safety and avoiding accidents.

Items Please

☒ Send the class any old magazines that include pictures related to traffic.

☒ We would like a few old tricycle or bicycle parts.

 # Children's Activities

Trucking Trike

Display several tricycles and tricycle pictures for children to examine. Encourage them to crawl under the trikes and look from all sides. Have children compare and describe the different trikes aloud. Write on a chart what they report. Review with them the name of all the parts (handlebars, seat, pedals, tires, wheels, axle, and others). Show them reflectors and ask what they know about them. Honk several bicycle horns and ask about them. Wave a bicycle flag and ask why it is important. Explain how reflectors, horns, and flags are related to safety and may keep children from running in front of a trike. Also point out that these items may help bigger bikes see and avoid hitting trikes. Show children a variety of helmets and discuss how they protect the head.

Materials

several kinds of tricycles, a variety of reflectors, flags, helmets, different styles of horns, pictures of trikes, chart paper, marker

Other Ideas

- Help children attach reflectors and horns to tricycles.
- Include pictures of a bicycle, tandem bicycle, rickshaw, and unicycle in the display.
- Visit places that sell or fix bicycles.
- Visit places that sell tires, wheels, air pumps, reflectors, and horns.
- Read *D.W. Rides Again*, by Marc Brown (New York: Little Brown, 1993).

Signs, Signs

Display international traffic signs and ask children to tell you about them. Give small groups of children miniature signs and have them find a large matching one. Review with children what each sign means and what *international* means. Help them make traffic signs.

Materials

tricycle path traffic signs, miniature traffic signs, cardboard, ink pens, scissors, black paint markers, duct tape, PVC pipes, dowels, self-hardening clay for miniature bases, clear contact paper for durability, tempera paint (red, yellow, orange, white, and green)

Other Ideas

- Visit or invite a signmaker to talk about his/her job and give sign-making tips.
- Visit the city traffic sign storage facility.
- Visit a theater or other site that has colored lights.
- Take a walk to see traffic signs.

Crossing Guards at Work

Arrange for children to watch traffic safety helpers at work and to interview them afterwards. Prepare children by showing them things a crossing guard might use or wear and briefly explain what a crossing guard does. Let them know about the trip and help them think of questions they may want to ask. Take pictures of the event so children can recall more details.

Materials

stop sign, whistle, vest or uniform, camera, film

Other Ideas

- Invite a crossing guard to visit the class and demonstrate his/her work on the trike path.
- Read *Make Way for Ducklings*, by Robert McCloskey (New York: Viking, 1941).
- Talk about listening for cars and read *Polar Bear, Polar Bear, What Do You Hear?* by Bill Martin, Jr. and Eric Carle (New York: Holt, 1991).

Reflections

Show the children materials that reflect and let them examine them. Turn the lights out and provide flashlights to shine toward the reflectors and reflective clothing. Ask for ideas about how the reflectors keep them safe. Explain that it is difficult for drivers to see people and things outside the car, so it is important to help the drivers see us by being more visible.

Materials

reflectors, small mirrors, reflective clothing, glow-in-the-dark objects, flashlights

Other Ideas

- Visit a store that sells reflective clothing.
- Encourage children to explore reflective materials in the sun.
- Help children create a reflection show with music and colored lights.
- Read *The Very Lonely Firefly*, by Eric Carle (New York: Philomel, 1995).

Stop

Tell children that you are going to conduct an experiment to see how something works. Have half of the children walk on the trike path or other designated place and pretend they are cars. Give the older children balls and other obstacles to roll across the "street" while children acting as "cars" are passing by. Let children exchange roles.

Call everyone together to talk about the experience. Ask what happened. Find out if some balls were harder to see than others, and why. Establish if it was harder for some people to stop than for others, and why (Were they speeding?). Ask how they felt during the experiment. Stress that it is hard for cars to stop and it is harder for them to see small things and short people. Tell them they should not run into the street for a toy or pet and that it is better to stand and play far away from the street. Explain that they should never play near a car, even a parked car, since a driver who gets in may not see them.

Materials
medium and large balls

Other Ideas

- Let children ride tricycles instead of walking for the experiment.
- Let children sit on a trike and experience that it is harder to see toys that are small.
- Read *Wheels on the Bus*, by Maryann Kovalski (Boston: Joy Street, 1987).

Topic 3

I Always Wear My Seat Belt

Learning Objectives:

☑ Children will state how seat belts help keep us safe.

☑ Children will be able to buckle and unbuckle seat belts.

☑ Children will practice seat belt use when in a vehicle.

Each year the injuries and deaths of many children in vehicle accidents could be prevented with proper use of restraints, such as lap belts, shoulder belts, and car seats. While children may not understand how staying in the seat protects them, they may understand the consequences of not staying in their seat (hitting the dashboard, hitting the windshield, falling out of the car). Help children begin to understand these consequences and practice correct use of various child restraints during transportation (see Family Information and Activity Bulletin).

If a child is large enough to use a regular lap belt, fasten it snugly across the hips. Discourage children from scrunching down in the seat, since this places the belt too high and could cause an injury in a crash. If the child is in a seat with a lap belt and shoulder belt, attach both properly. A shoulder belt alone is not a proper restraint.

Never place a child in a car seat in the front passenger seat if the vehicle has passenger-side air bags. Air bags are designed to save lives by inflating and forming a cushion of air for an individual who is properly buckled. In a crash, the air bag will inflate with extreme speed and force. A child in a car seat or an unbuckled child or adult will be too close to the inflating air bag and can be severely injured or killed by the impact. Until children are large enough to wear a lap and shoulder belt properly, place them in the rear seat if the vehicle is equipped with an air bag.

Creating the Environment

Provide belts of all kinds for children to practice buckling and unbuckling. If possible, provide seat belts of the type found in most vehicles. When children are transported, vehicles should have seat belts and car seats for younger children. Strollers, high chairs, child seats and carriers, and playground swings with safety seats for very young children are all examples of ways to help keep children safe from falls and other injuries.

Transportation safety is also influenced by the type and maintenance of the vehicle and the driver's training and qualifications. Check state regulations to ensure compliance.

Evaluation:

☒ Are children discussing the use of seat belts?

☒ Are children able to buckle and unbuckle seat belts?

☒ Do children practice wearing their seat belts?

Family Information & Activity

Bulletin

I Always Wear My Seat Belt

Motor vehicle accidents are a leading cause of injury, brain and spinal cord damage, and death for young children. If seat belts are not used, a crash at only 5 miles per hour can send your child crashing into the dashboard or windshield.

The safest place for your child is the center of the back seat. Older children should wear lap and shoulder belts, while young children are much safer in a car seat. Keep the following guidelines in mind: 1) A car seat may be designed for infants, toddlers, or larger children. Be sure the seat is designed or adjusted for the size/age of your child. 2) If your vehicle has dual air bags, never place your child in a car seat or booster seat in the front passenger side. 3) Infants should be placed in rear-facing car seats. If the car seat is designed for it, toddlers and preschoolers may face forward. 4) Secure the seat in the car. Adjust and secure the straps to fit your child. 5) Children are more likely to buckle up if they see you buckle up.

Family Activities

☒ Take a walk through your home and look for all kinds of belts. Talk about their purpose.

☒ Make it a family habit and rule that everyone wears a seat belt during car trips.

Ideas Please

☒ Tell us places to go or people to see that might help children learn about car safety.

Items Please

☒ Old seat belts are needed for practicing.

☒ Send us old belts, rope, hooks, and other things that fasten.

Children's Activities

Belts Galore

Gather a wide variety of belts. Put belts in a large basket and invite children to examine them. Encourage children to describe the belts and compare them. Have them sort the belts many ways (length, width, material, color, buckle). Let children try the belts on and practice buckling them. Ask why people wear belts. See if they can think of other kinds of belts. If they do not mention seat belts, point out that people wear seat belts too, and ask if they know why.

Note: Some families may use a belt to discipline children; therefore, belts may be frightening.

Materials

belts with bells, with tassels and sequins and a variety of buckles (brass, silver, square, round, or cloth-covered buckles), belts of many colors (brown, tan, black, green, white, multicolored, red, clear), belts made different ways (braided, rope, leather, suede, bead, chain, terry cloth, elastic, silk)

Other Ideas

- Let children make belts.
- Visit a belt factory.
- Invite families to share information about a meaningful belt.
- Encourage children to find and cut out pictures of belts to glue on to a box.

Belt Detective

Show children some objects that have belts and talk about why they have them. Ask the children to think of other objects that might have belts. Encourage them to search for other belts in the room, their homes, outside, and every place they go. Ask the children to report on all of the belts they find and what the belts were holding.

Materials

belted objects (suitcase, backpack, high chair, car seat, stroller, amusement park rides, coats, airplanes)

Other Ideas

- Let children use a luggage cart and "tie-down" to transport boxes.
- Visit a store to see all the belted items they have.
- Introduce and add car seats to the dramatic play area.

Seat Belt Beginning

Before this activity, obtain a vehicle seat belt from the police department, traffic safety school, an automobile salvage lot, or car garage. Show children a vehicle seat belt and ask them to tell you what they know about it. Write down what the children say. Let children examine and practice with the belt. Stress how important it is for them to wear their seat belts. Tell them that they will get to practice with more seat belts later.

Materials

seat belt, chalkboard, chalk

Other Ideas

- Assist children in creating a vehicle that has seat belts using boxes, chairs, and belts.

- Look at seat belts in a car and ask children what they know about the belts.

- Show children pictures of seat belts and encourage discussion.

Seat Belt Marathon

Arrange a trip to a car dealership and let children examine seat belts, car seats, shoulder straps, and air bag spaces in many different vehicles. While at the car dealership, children can practice buckling and unbuckling seat belts in front and back seats. Help children learn to move the front seat away from the dashboard. Take pictures of the experience so children can reflect upon it. Help children write and illustrate a thank-you note to the dealership after the trip. See if the dealer would like you to invite the media to the "Seat Belt Marathon." The coverage would be a great thank-you to the dealer and serve as an excellent public service announcement about the importance of buckling up.

Materials

camera, film, construction paper, paint, markers

Other Ideas

- Visit an airport to see seat belts and hear the preflight information about seat belts.

- Visit a bus station to see if buses have seat belts.

- Visit a train station to learn about the seating.

- Play "Come Take a Trip In My Airship," by Natalie Merchant (*For Our Children Too!* Rhino, 72494).

Underneath

Arrange for children to visit a car service garage or body shop and examine how seat belts are connected to the vehicles. Ask if children can observe as a seat belt is removed or replaced. Observe and learn about any tools that are used. Look at a car that has a seat belt removed and assist the children in asking questions that interest them. Videotape the children researching seat belts. While there, look at wrecked vehicles and talk with children about any experiences they have had with wrecks. Help children create a thank-you note and send it to the shop.

Materials

video camera, film, art materials

Other Ideas

- Invite someone to visit and tell about how seat belts are connected to cars.

- Visit an auto manufacturing plant to watch the assembly of seats and seat belts.

- Examine vehicles at school to see how seat belts are connected.

- Play "Bumping Up and Down," by Raffi (*Singable Songs for the Very Young*. Shoreline, 10037).

Topic 4
Stay Away From Weapons

Learning objectives:

☑ Children will identify peaceful ways to resolve conflict.

☑ Children will recognize weapons.

☑ Children will state what to do if they find a weapon.

☑ Children will tell about the different purposes for which weapons are used.

Violence and availability of weapons has become an issue that many young children face in our society. The purpose of this unit is to teach children to avoid dangers associated with weapons.

Determine what weapons (rifles, handguns, knives, bow and arrows) are prevalent in your community and what dangers young children may face (finding a gun in a closet, drive-by shootings, gang violence). It is helpful when staff know their community and risks and parents are involved in this discussion. Provide children with factual information regarding weapons and what they should do if they find one. If children find a weapon, they should tell an adult, lead the adult to the location, and point to (not touch) the weapon.

Care should be given not to frighten children unnecessarily or use negative labels, such as "bad guys," when referring to people who carry or use weapons. Children may be exposed to weapons in a variety of ways. They may come in contact with military and police personnel, hunters, or gun collectors. Help children understand that it is not wrong for an adult to own a weapon, but that children and adults can be hurt by weapons when they are not used safely. Children may also encounter individuals with intent to hurt others. Children watch television and movies that have weapons in them, and they may see them in their home, at a friend's home, or in the community.

Too often children do not comprehend the difference between a toy and a real gun. They may play with a toy weapon, only to learn too late that it is real. This topic teaches that all weapons should be considered real and should be avoided by children. For children to avoid potential hazards, they must first recognize the hazard. Depending upon the community or culture, children may be exposed to BB guns, hunting rifles, knives, swords, or military weapons, such as grenades.

Creating the Environment

Weapons, including replicas or pictures of weapons, are not appropriate for school use except when teaching about safety. Teachers may use pictures or replicas in small-group discussions, but should not leave items out for free play or learning center time. If replicas are used as a teaching tool, they should be shown to the children by the teacher, but the children should not be allowed to touch the replicas. This reinforces the idea that children should not touch weapons.

Evaluation:

- ☒ Are children talking about and asking questions regarding weapons?
- ☒ Do children show an understanding of what to do if they find a weapon?
- ☒ Are children discussing or displaying peaceful resolutions to conflicts?

Family Information & Activity Bulletin

Stay Away From Weapons

Each year, 24,000 children are injured by guns, and approximately 230 children are killed. Children may come across weapons at home, at a friend's house, or even on a playground. In communities near military bases, children may find explosives, such as hand grenades. A child may play with a toy gun or hand grenade only to learn too late that it is real.

Teach your child that all weapons should be considered real and should be avoided. This includes guns, military weapons, hunting knives, bows and arrows, mace and pepper spray, or other weapons.

The rule in weapon safety is "Don't touch a weapon!" If children find a weapon, they should go tell an adult, then point to (not touch) the weapon. All weapons should be stored in a locked cabinet or closet, with ammunition stored separately.

Family Activities

- ☒ Talk to your child about weapons and share your beliefs and values.
- ☒ Watch and discuss with your child any TV shows you allow them to watch that contain weapons.

Ideas Please

- ☒ Give us your ideas for guest speakers that can help your child learn to avoid weapons.

Items Please

- ☒ Send the class any old magazines that include pictures of weapons.

DON'T TOUCH

Children's Activities

Clap and Stomp

Begin clapping your hands. Invite children to clap along with you. Start stomping your feet and encourage children to stomp. Introduce a fast and lively song to encourage children's dancing and clapping. After the song, ask children for other words that describe what they were doing. Explain that although this activity was fun and no one was hurt, sometimes hitting and slapping hurts. Ask children to recall any time when they have seen people hit someone. Encourage them to talk about things they can do instead of hitting when they are mad or upset. Reassure children who are fearful.

Materials
dancing music, tape or CD player

Other Ideas

- Visit or invite a conflict resolution counselor or peace advocate.
- Play "Clap Your Hands" by Tickle Tune Typhoon (*Circle Around.* Tickle Tune Typhoon Records).

Hit and Shake

Invite children to select various percussion instruments to play and march to the music. After children have returned their instruments, ask them to describe what they were doing. Prompt children to describe the activity with words like "hit" and "shake." Tell children that you think it is fun to play instruments by hitting and shaking them. Ask what they think about using the instruments to hit someone. Tell them that objects used to hurt people are called "weapons," and ask if they have heard the word. Explain that, although someone could hit with a musical instrument, it is not called a weapon unless it is used in that way.

Materials
marching music, multicultural rhythm instruments, tape or CD player

Other Ideas

- Let children make instruments to hit and shake. Discuss hitting and shaking.
- Play music and let children shake their different body parts. Discuss the difference in shaking your own body and shaking someone else's.
- Play "Shake Your Brains," by Red Grammar (*Teaching Peace.* Children's Group, 4202).

Picturing Weapons

Show children pictures of weapons and ask them to tell you about them. Explain that you wanted to show them pictures to be sure they knew what they looked like. Tell them they should not touch a weapon if they see one, but they should tell an adult. Ask them to name some adults they could tell. Let the children look for pictures of weapons and cut or tear them out. Help the children make puzzles by pasting the pictures onto cardboard and then cutting them into puzzle pieces.

Materials

pictures of weapons, magazines, catalogues, cardboard, paste, scissors, envelope for storing puzzle piece

Other Ideas

- Visit a store that sells weapons.
- Visit a store that sells gun cabinets and cases for safe storage.
- Play "Aiye Mire," by Babatundi Olatunji (*Peace is the World Smiling.* Music for Little People, 2104).

Helpful Ways

Show children pictures of weapons and ask for ways weapons are used that might be helpful. Examples might include a knife used to cut food, a gun used by a police officer or soldier to help keep us safe, a gun or bow and arrow used to hunt animals for food, dynamite used to clear rock for a new road, a cannon used at a football game to celebrate points made. During conversation, point out that, although some people use weapons in useful ways, they are not for children. Remind them not to touch a weapon, and to tell an adult if they see one.

Materials

pictures of weapons mounted on cardboard

Other Ideas

- Visit or invite a solider or police officer to talk about how they use weapons and why.
- Visit or invite someone who hunts animals for food.
- Visit or invite a woodcarver or someone who whittles.
- Visit or invite a chef to talk about the use of knives in food preparation.
- Play "Kids' Peace Song," by Peter Alsop (*Peace is the World Smiling.* Music for Little People, 2104).

No Flying Weapon

Tell children that adults have rules too. Adults are not allowed to take weapons some places, like on airplanes. Hold up a toy airplane and explain that before you ride on an airplane, you must go through a metal detector so guards can check for weapons. Explain that it is just like walking through a door and does not hurt. Announce if you will be visiting an airport to see one.

Materials

toy airplane

Other Ideas

- After the airport trip, help children develop a replica of a metal detector.
- Visit an alternative site that has metal detectors.
- Set up a model metal detector for children instead of going to see one.

Topic 5
Get Away From Fire

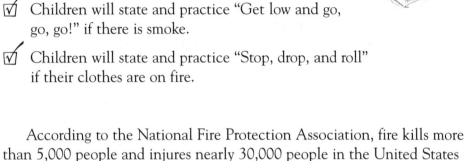

Learning Objectives:

☑ Children will practice what to do if they hear a smoke detector alarm.

☑ Children will identify routes and exits out of their classroom or home.

☑ Children will state and practice "Get low and go, go, go!" if there is smoke.

☑ Children will state and practice "Stop, drop, and roll" if their clothes are on fire.

According to the National Fire Protection Association, fire kills more than 5,000 people and injures nearly 30,000 people in the United States every year. Fire and burns are the third leading cause of death for young children in the United States. Preschool children are more than twice as likely as older children or adults to die in a fire.

Young children often die in fires because they don't know what to do. Children may not understand that fire can go anywhere, and they may try to hide from it. Children may be afraid of firefighters because of their protective clothing and gear. It is essential that teachers evaluate each child's knowledge and skill in this area, and provide additional learning activities as needed to assure that all children meet the objectives.

A picture of a person with their clothing on fire may be disturbing to some children. Instead, show a picture of an item of clothing on fire, such as a shirt, or hold a picture of flames up to clothing. Teach children the seriousness of fire safety without frightening them.

One of the most common causes of deadly fires is children playing with such objects as candles, matches, hot water heaters, space heaters, stoves, lighters, and flammable liquids. Other causes include combustible items being placed too close to a heat source or flame; neglected appliances and electrical items (which may have frayed cords and wiring shorts); careless use of cigarettes or other smoking materials; and leaving heating equipment, such as space heaters and fireplaces, unattended.

Adults should understand proper storage of flammable materials such as grease, gasoline, and paint thinner. Check with your local fire department for more information.

In addition to fire prevention and safety, staff should discuss burn prevention with children and parents. Children can receive serious burns in just a few seconds from a hot iron, hot foods, or even tap water. (See the "Resources" section for information on the Learn Not to Burn preschool curriculum.)

Creating the Environment

Every facility should have working smoke detectors, a fire alarm system, accessible fire extinguishers, fire doors, and several exit routes. Post fire escape routes by the classroom door for staff to memorize. Practice fire drills to avoid confusion in the case of an actual emergency.

Carefully check the classroom and playground for fire and burn hazards. If extension cords must be used, regularly inspect them for signs of wear, and position the extension chords so children cannot pull them or trip over them. Never place an electrical cord under a rug or carpet. Cover electrical outlets when not in use. Tap water should be checked to assure that it is not above 120° Fahrenheit. Carefully supervise cooking activities that require the use of electrical appliances or result in hot foods. Add props like pot holders and smoke alarms to learning centers to encourage fire safety.

Evaluation:

☒ During role-playing, are children including evacuation action?

☒ Are children discussing fire?

☒ Are children able to state what to do in case of a drill or fire?

☒ Are children participating in fire drills and practice activities?

Family Information & Activity Bulletin

Get Away From Fire

In just 30 seconds, a small flame from a dropped match can become a fire burning out of control. Install smoke detectors on the ceiling or high on the wall on each floor in your home, close to bedrooms, and at the top of stairs. Test the smoke detectors often and change the batteries at least once each year.

Things your child can learn to do in case of fire include the following:

- "Don't hide from fire!" Get out of the house!

- "Stop, drop, and roll" if your clothes catch on fire.

- "Get low and go, go, go!" if there is smoke.

- Know emergency exits and go to them when there is a fire.

- Practice opening a locked window. Show your child how to push out a screen. If the window is a few feet above the ground, show them how to hang from their hands and drop to the ground. Choose a safe meeting place outside where everyone should go.

Family Activities

- ☒ Make it a family habit to practice various escape plans from your home in case of fire.

- ☒ Establish a schedule for changing batteries in fire alarms twice a year. Pick dates easy to remember, like birthdays or other events.

Ideas Please

- ☒ Tell us your ideas for activities relating to fire safety and prevention.

Items Please

- ☒ Send the class any old magazines that include pictures related to fire and fire safety.

- ☒ We could also use fire extinguishers and smoke detectors that no longer work. Children will examine them.

Children's Activities

The Heat Is On

Provide something warm for children to feel and talk about, like a heating pad, a coin in the sun, or a muffin fresh out of the oven. Ask children if they can remember a time when something warm felt good to them. See if children can remember a time when something was too warm and it hurt to touch it. Discuss getting burned and how to avoid it.

Ask children how they think things get warm or hot. Talk about different ways to get something hot, such as plugging it in or puting it in the oven.

Let each child select an object to take outside to put in the sun. Help children write their names on pieces of paper to be placed near or taped to their objects. Encourage children to check on them and talk about their findings.

Safety Note: Ensure that what children feel is not hot. Do not leave a heating pad plugged in or unattended. Children should wash and dry their hands before the activity. Check for appropriate temperature before initiating the outside sunning portion of this activity.

Materials

objects selected by children, paper, pen, tape, warm object to feel (water, warm hand cloth, hot water bottle, heating pad, or bed buddy)

Other Ideas

- Have children select from predetermined objects for sunning.
- Let children briefly place objects in warm water and check how they feel.
- Invite children to feel ice cubes and a warm object and compare the experience.
- Have children use thermometers to check the temperature of different places.
- Visit a glass blower to see the creations and watch how fire is used.
- Visit a candle maker to observe and ask questions.

By the Light of the Fire

Introduce and play Native American flute songs as a calming activity. Tell children that you are going to light a fire (a candle or oil lamp), and that it is important they stay behind the line you have made. Walk around the line and demonstrate where children are to stay. Explain that you want to show them a flame, but they need to know that children should not start fires because it is too dangerous.

After you light the fire, ask children to talk about times they have seen a fire. Ask if they have seen lighted candles at home or on a cake. Tell the children that some people use candles to celebrate special events. Ask if they can think of a way heat is used to help us. Help children understand that heat is used to cook and keep homes warm. Thank children for staying safe and let them know that you are blowing the flame out.

Safety Note: Be sure there is adequate supervision for this activity. Test the candle or lamp prior to the activity. A physical reminder of the boundary is important. With close guidance, children can learn appropriate behavior around fire. Exposure to planned and supervised situations give children the opportunity to practice skills.

Materials

candle or oil lamp, masking tape or rope to show boundaries, Native American flute music (such as *Dream Catchers,* by Tokeya Inajin, EarthBeat! 2696)

Other Ideas

- Instead of a fire, use a lamp with a flame-shaped bulb.
- Learn about lights used during Hanukkah, winter solstice, or other celebrations.
- Read *Seven Candles For Kwanzaa,* by Andrea Davis Pinkney (New York: Dial, 1993) and talk about how candles are used.

Fire Alarm and Drill

Show children pictures or a videotape of fires, and tell them that sometimes fire gets too big and is hard to stop. Hold up a smoke detector and see if the children know what it is. Have several available for them to examine. Tell them that we need to practice some procedures so we are ready if there is a fire. Let children hear a variety of alarms. Announce that when they hear a sound like these, they should stop playing and go outside with a teacher. Give each child a copy of a map showing their exit route from the building. Follow map directions with them to show them where to go if they hear the alarm. Have several practice drills using different exits available, including windows.

Materials
pictures or video of fire, VCR and monitor, several working smoke detectors with different sounds

Other Ideas
- Arrange for children to watch an older class having a fire drill.
- Visit a business that sells fire alarm system to see and hear many alarms and other supplies.
- Involve children in drawing an emergency exit floor plan.
- Look for exit signs and talk about why they are posted.
- Invite family members to visit and tell about their home emergency exit plans.
- Have a picnic and let children see the fire in the grill.

Smoke

Ask children to hold a parachute or bedsheet "up high," "medium," and "down low." Repeat these actions a few times. Place a ball on the parachute for them to roll. Roll a ball under the parachute, then let several children roll the ball under the parachute. Ask for volunteers to take the ball and crawl under to the other side. Encourage each child to try crawling under the parachute, with or without the ball, and with or without a friend. After the children have all had a turn, have them sit with you so you can show them pictures of smoke. Invite them to discuss the pictures. Tell them that, in case of smoke, they need to "Get low and go, go, go!" Have children chant "Get low and go, go, go!" with you. As a group, practice quickly crawling to the door. Let the children practice crawling under the parachute again, pretending that it is smoke.

Materials
parachute, balls, pictures of smoke

Other Ideas
- Let children use tissue paper and poster board to create smoke they can practice crawling under, or let them practice crawling through large boxes.
- Teach children the limbo.
- Visit a room that has a fireplace and investigate.
- Talk with someone who cleans chimneys and find out why chimneys need cleaning.
- Read and discuss *Fire, Fire Said Mrs. McGuire*, by Bill Martin, Jr. (New York: Holt, 1970).

Flames

Show children a rolling pin and how it works. See how many other things they can name that roll, such as balls, tires, and bottles. Ask for volunteers to roll their bodies. Let all the children who are interested show you how they can crawl. Help those who have difficulty. Show children pictures of clothes (not people) that are on fire and tell the children that if their clothes ever catch on fire they should "Stop, drop, and roll." Show them how to do this as you say it. Have them practice chanting it with you. Follow-up at later times to help them remember.

Materials
rolling pin, pictures of clothes on fire

Other Ideas
- Tell children to find something in the room that rolls and bring it to group time to show.
- Provide playdough and a variety of rolling pins for children to use and discuss.
- Let children roll on a variety of surfaces, like grass, carpet, pillows, and tile. Discuss how each surface feels.

Chapter 7

If I Need Help

Young children look to adults, including parents, teachers, baby sitters, or other responsible adults, to take care of them. Helping children become familiar with the roles of various health and safety workers may help children feel more comfortable with these individuals.

In a fire emergency, children may be frightened of the firefighter who has on a helmet, uniform, and oxygen tank. Children may fear police officers if they are regularly exposed to violence, if members of their family or race are frequently discriminated against, or if they live with an adult involved in illegal activities. Children who are hurt or who have an injured loved one may not understand that paramedics can help them, or that it is okay to go in an ambulance.

The goal of this theme is to help children realize that health and safety workers can assist them, and that children should ask for their help, if needed. The activities and resources presented will introduce habits that may help prevent injury or death by encouraging children to seek appropriate assistance, help children begin to recognize the role of health and safety helpers, and foster positive feelings about community health and safety personnel.

Addressing Diversity

The history families have with emergency and safety workers, combined with the environment they live in, may influence how this theme is received. Family beliefs about illness and treatment may vary widely. Individualizing this theme for the children's situations and the community where they live is necessary to avoid fear, confusion, and hostility.

Use appropriate and inclusive language that does not specify gender. For example, instead of "fireman" say "firefighter." Include materials and guest speakers that are representative of various cultures and both genders to facilitate trust.

Where Will the Theme Lead?

Use these words to stimulate ideas for follow-up activities:

immunization	disaster	pediatrician	paramedics	detective
filling	locksmith	treatment	wound	trauma
stretcher	barricade	riot	contagious	ambulance
investigate	breathing	mud slide	chiropractor	shock
hydrant	apparatus	emergency exit	rescue	alert
siren	arson	water patrol	drill	911

Learning Center Materials

Dramatic Play:
plastic raincoats, helmets, boots
first-aid book, bandages, tape, child scissors, antiseptic wipes, cotton, plastic gloves, tweezers, ice pack, thermometer strip, stethoscope
many kinds of telephones
phone book with safety numbers highlighted
eyeglass frames and eye chart
safety and health uniforms

Table Toys:
miniature fire and rescue vehicles
emergency worker and vehicle puzzles
cotton balls and tweezers
pictures of emergency workers cut in strips
building sets with wheels
building sets for hospitals
health worker puzzles
number puzzles (911)
badges to sort

Language Arts:
puppets of emergency or healthcare worker
flannel board and emergency worker set
telephone, message pad, pencil
telephone book
first-aid book and charts
fire emergency cards from hotels
clipboard with paper and pen for chart
job application forms
doctor's appointment book
chalkboard and chalk

Science:
many kinds of flashlights
telephone to take apart
hose nozzles to examine
dental tools to examine
stethoscope
eyeglass frames and small screwdriver
earplugs
hearing aids
first-aid kit

Blocks:

emergency vehicles and workers
cotton balls to haul
pictures of fire departments, police stations, and hospitals to post
caution and danger signs
first-aid tape to hold blocks together
tongue depressors
figures of safety and healthcare workers
red tissue paper

Art:

emergency vehicles for models
plastic badges for tracing or gluing
small pieces of tubing or hose
pictures of safety personnel cut into squares for gluing
red tissue paper
cotton swabs for gluing or painting
plastic gloves for puppet making
first-aid tape

Outside:
ropes
boxes to become vehicles or houses
small ladder
hose
stretcher and blanket
walkie-talkies
emergency signs to add to vehicles
telephone
large chalk

Library Books:
Barney is Best, by Nancy White Carlstrom (New York: Harper, 1994).
Daddies at Work, by Eve Merriam (New York: Simon and Schuster, 1989).
Mommies at Work, by Eve Merriam (New York: Simon and Schuster, 1989).
The Checkup, by Helen Oxenbury (New York: Dial, 1983).

Topic 1

People Who Help Me Take Care of My Body

Learning Objectives:

☑ Children will identify different people who are health helpers.

☑ Children will identify places where doctors, nurses, and other health personnel work.

☑ Children will state why people might need to see a doctor or nurse, or go to a hospital.

Family beliefs and customs vary greatly regarding when and what type of medical attention to seek. Work with families to identify and support the individual needs of each child. Extend invitations to family members in the healthcare field to be guest speakers.

When gathering materials or deciding on field trips and guest speakers, include doctors and nurses from many specialties, lab technicians, paramedics, health educators, dentists, eye doctors, and school nurses. Try to include some medical specialties that might be less familiar, such as chiropractors, acupuncturists, and podiatrists. Information provided should contain references and facts regarding where these people work, such as a doctor's office, school, hospital, clinic, dental trailer, and health department.

As children explore the roles of healthcare professionals and hear about what they do, begin to talk about occasions when this type of help might be needed. Present the topic honestly, but be careful not to frighten children. Allow ample time for children to process, role-play, and ask questions.

Provide opportunities for healthcare workers to visit the classroom as guest speakers so that children can see them in a familiar environment. Later, provide additional opportunities to see the same professionals, and others, in their various health-related environments.

Creating the Environment

Expose children to materials and equipment related to healthcare fields, such as uniforms, stethoscopes, bandages, cotton balls, and eye charts. Extend learning by inviting a variety of health-related guest speakers of various race and gender, and by taking field trips to visit healthcare professionals on location.

Evaluation:

☒ During role-playing, are children acting out health-related issues?

☒ During conversation, are children using health-related vocabulary?

☒ Can children answer questions about when a doctor or nurse might be needed?

Family Information & Activity Bulletin

People Who Help Me Take Care of My Body

Talk to your child before going for healthcare. Help your child understand that doctors and nurses help people feel better. Talk about any fears your child may have. Try not to scare your child, but be honest. Take a favorite toy, a book, or crayons and paper along so your child can play while waiting or receiving care. A favorite doll or blanket often helps. Make a list of your child's symptoms, such as fever, and how long the symptoms have been present. Once the doctor has assessed your child's health, ask questions such as: 1) What is the name of the illness or condition? How long will it last? 2) What are the options for treatment and their side effects?

3) What other symptoms should I expect or watch for, and how long will they last? 4) Is the condition contagious? Can my child go back to day care or school with this condition? 5) What can I do to prevent reoccurrence?

Family Activities

☒ Let your child find magazine pictures of healthcare workers, such as doctors, nurses, and dentists, and cut each picture into puzzle pieces for your child to put together.

☒ Share with your child your family experiences with health helpers.

Ideas Please

☒ Give us ideas to help children learn about people working in the health field.

☒ Please let us know about any experiences with health professionals or family beliefs about medical and dental care that may make this topic confusing or upsetting to your child.

Items Please

☒ We need lots of pictures of doctors, dentists, nurses, medical supplies or equipment, hospitals, or anything else related to healthcare workers.

Children's Activities

Health Helping Hands

Ask children to tell about the kind of jobs their family members have. Tell children that some jobs involve helping others stay safe and healthy. Invite people from city emergency rooms, health and safety departments, and support service agencies to visit the class and explain how they contribute to our health. Examples of people to invite include emergency medical technicians, health department medical staff, hospital medical staff, mental health professionals, lifeguards, sanitation workers, and animal shelter workers. Ask them to explain not only what they do to help, but where they work and how they can be reached when help is needed. To help children understand, encourage guests to bring printed materials, pictures, and tools used on the job. Printed information that visitors bring can be included in a "health helpers" scrapbook, notebook, display, or on a bulletin board. After the visit, involve children in writing thank-you notes. Write a brief report about the visits and submit it to a newsletter or community paper.

Materials

glue and tape, hole punch, notebook or scrapbook, paper and ink, pens

Other Ideas

- Introduce different healthcare workers and related tools daily using puzzles, puppets, and books.
- Read *What I Want To Be*, by P. Mignon Hinds (New York: Western, 1995).

Far and Near

When children are outside, ask them to face one direction and look at the things they can see. Write down the things they list. Provide tools to enhance sight (binoculars, magnifier, microscope, and telescope) and ask them to look again and tell what they see. Make a new list and talk about the differences. Explain that we all use tools to help us see sometimes, and that some people use these tools to see all the time. Show eyeglasses and ask what the children know about them.

Materials

paper, marker, magnifier, binoculars, microscope, telescope, periscope, camera with zoom lens

Other Ideas

- Explain about eye doctors and exams. Tell the children that eye doctors have different machines to look through than the ones they are using.

- To practice for an eye exam, give each child a paper doll and ask them to turn it like you turn your paper doll. Hold the doll upright, to the left, upside down, and to the right.
- Post an eye exam chart for role-playing.
- Visit an ophthalmologist and let children see the equipment and ask questions.
- Let a child who has had a screening or exam tell about it.
- Set up an eye doctor office as a special learning center.
- Read *William and the Good Old Days,* by Eloise Greenfield (New York: Harper, 1993).

A Little Softer Now

Tell children that soft sounds are restful and help people relax. Ask children to watch and listen to you clap your hands. Stand up and clap really loud, bend down and clap a little softer, and then sit down and clap very softly. Repeat, and then invite children to clap with you. Teach children to watch your hand and to clap loud when it is high and to get softer as it gets lower. Try slowly moving from loud to soft, and also try quickly jumping from loud to soft. Sing a song loudly, then softer and softer, until you and the children are only moving your lips and there is no sound. This technique can be used with other songs, instruments, finger plays, or chants to get children focused and ready to listen. End by playing soft music for children to listen to and relax.

Materials

tape or CD player, "Brahms' Lullaby," by Celine Dion (*For Our Children Too!* Rhino, 72494)

Other Ideas

- Explain that some people have a harder time hearing than others, and that it is important for everyone to get their hearing checked to see how well they can hear.
- Practice hearing exams by having children take turns using headphones. Ask children to raise their hands when they hear something. Turn music on softly and watch for their signal.
- Visit a hearing exam lab and look at the equipment.
- Let a child who has had a hearing exam tell about it.
- Set up a hearing exam lab as a special learning center.
- Play "Let's Make Some Noise," by Raffi (*Everything Grows.* Shoreline, 10039).

Dog Days

Arrange for a good-natured dog, one accustomed to young children, to visit the classroom. Prior to the visit, ask children to talk about what they think dog's teeth will look like. Suggest that they draw a picture of what the dog teeth may look like. When the dog arrives, have a few children at a time look closely at the teeth. Encourage them to bring their drawing of dog teeth close to the dog so they can see how close their prediction was. Children may be interested in drawing another picture to more accurately reflect the dog teeth after they have seen them. Involve children in sending a dog bone or biscuit and thank-you note to the dog and owner.

Safety Note: Even gentle dogs can become aggressive when frightened. Be sure to prepare children about how to approach the dog. Limit the number of children who can approach the dog at a time, and have an adult overseeing the dog at all times.

Materials

gentle dog, paper, pencil

Other Ideas

- Explain that dentists look at people's teeth, just like the children looked at the dog's teeth. Let them know that dentists are checking to see if the teeth are healthy or need to be fixed.

- Visit a dentist office to meet the dentist and see the equipment.

- Set up a dentist office as a special learning center.

- Play "Brush Your Teeth," by Raffi (*Singable Songs for the Very Young.* Shoreline, 10037).

Animal Bodies

Give each child in the group a stuffed animal to hold. Ask how the stuffed animals are alike. Ask additional questions to help children see that all of the animals have bodies and body parts similar to people. Point out the differences in people parts and animal parts, such as hands and paws. Let children name the differences they see. Ask children to check their animal's sight, hearing, and teeth. Have them also check their animal's body to see if everything is all right. The pulse, temperature, blood pressure, and reflexes can be checked. Give them a notepad to record the results, and have them show it to you after they have finished.

Safety Note: Check all stuffed animals to ensure that there are no loose parts that children could dislodge, insert in their mouths, and choke on.

Materials
stuffed animals, notepad, ink pen, wooden mallet, thermometer strip, stethoscope, blood pressure cuff

Other Ideas
- Visit a doctors office, hospital, or health department to learn about what happens during a physical.
- Invite a doctor to the classroom to tell about a checkup.
- Let children check their own sight, hearing, teeth, pulse, temperature, blood pressure, and reflexes.

Topic 2
Who Takes Care of Me

Learning Objectives:

☑ Children will identify safety helpers.

☑ Children will identify situations when they might need help.

☑ Children will practice calling 911 and answering the questions 911 personnel may ask.

Who children should turn to for help will be based on resources available in the community and is a family decision. The types of emergencies that children and families might encounter will differ depending on the demographics and geographic location; thus, the focus of this topic should be meaningful to your area. If flooding is a frequent event, spend more time helping children prepare for and deal with flooding than other situations. The provided activities address more universal emergencies and will need to be supplemented.

Without invading family privacy, gather information about critical events the children have witnessed or experienced. Individual support can be offered and activities can be modified as needed. Be aware that not all children have telephones in their homes.

Many individuals, organizations, and businesses related to emergency situations could be included in classroom curriculum. For example, businesses that provide supplies for firefighters, volunteers, insurance companies, construction workers, and cleaning businesses that provide services after fires or floods may all provide different perspectives on safety.

Note: When discussing fire, be sure to emphasize getting out of the burning house and then calling 911 from a neighbor's house.

Creating the Environment

Include many kinds of phones on which children can practice. Check local emergency facilities to see if a 911 simulation is available for loan to help children become comfortable. Provide pictures and equipment related to the various safety helper roles for children to view and incorporate into their role-playing. Extend learning by inviting guest speakers who have safety roles, and use field trips to visit the safety-related environments of guests and other safety helpers.

Evaluation:

☒ Are children role-playing various safety helpers?

☒ During conversations, are children talking about safety helpers?

☒ Can children dial 911?

Family Information & Activity

Bulletin

Who Takes Care of Me

Most illnesses and injuries are not true emergencies; however, bleeding, an inability to breathe, and poisoning are three "hurry" cases. **Bleeding:** A child can bleed to death in less than one minute if a large vein or artery is cut. If your child is bleeding, apply direct pressure to stop it. If the blood does not stop in 5 to 10 minutes, or if it is spurting out, get immediate medical help. **Breathing:** A child can have permanent brain damage in 4 minutes if breathing stops. A child who is having a hard time breathing and whose lips, skin, or fingernails look blue is not getting enough oxygen. If a child cannot cough, speak, or breathe, call 911! **Poisoning:** Poisons eaten or breathed can be deadly in just a few minutes. If you think your child has swallowed or breathed poison, call the poison control center in your area and they will tell you what to do. Keep the poison control center number posted by your telephone. Serious burns and head, neck, and back injuries also need immediate medical help.

Family Activities

☒ Talk to your child about community safety workers and your experiences with them.

☒ Tell your child how to get help in an emergency, and help them practice making the contact.

Ideas Please

☒ Give us the titles of any books that might help children learn how to get help if they need it.

Items Please

☒ Send the class any old magazines, flyers, or greeting cards with pictures of community safety helpers, such as firefighters, police officers, rescue workers, and Red Cross volunteers.

©1997 Redleaf Press, *Growing, Growing Strong*

Children's Activities

Solving the Puzzle

In a small group, give each child a piece of a puzzle that represents a community safety helper in your community. Tell children to work on the puzzle together. Ask them what they know about that helper. Have them gather information related to this worker. Help them prepare and share information with the large group about that helper. Take pictures of children giving their report and send it to the local community, the safety helpers represented, and to the newspaper.

Materials

camera and film, puzzles of safety helpers in your community (firefighter, police officer, paramedic, crossing guard, sea rescuer, pilot, National Guard, Red Cross volunteer), classroom supplies about the same helpers (books, music, puppets, play people, pictures, games)

Other Ideas

- Involve families by having children gather information from them before sharing with the other children.
- Take photographs of actual safety workers, mount them on cardboard, and cut into puzzles to use.
- Invite family members to visit and share stories about how safety helpers have helped their family.
- Invite people from the city emergency and safety departments to visit.

Fighting Fire

Arrange for a field trip to the local fire station so children can see the tools and clothes used by firefighters. Before the trip, make a list of what children want to learn about and questions they may want to ask. Encourage children to draw, trace, or copy interesting things they see on the trip. Videotape the experience so children can review it and family members can see it. Contact the local media to see if they can cover the trip. Coverage will help the community learn about your class and call attention to fire prevention.

Materials

children's questions, paper, ballpoint pens, video camera and blank tape

Other Ideas

- After the trip, invite children to represent what they saw through art, construction, or dramatic play.

- As a thank-you, assist children in making a class book to show what they learned, and send it to the firefighters.

- Let children make firefighter puppets.

Police Please

Before this activity, take pictures and develop slides of many different police officers, representing as much diversity as possible. Introduce the slide show and ask children what they think the police officers will look like. Tell them to watch to see all the ways police officers can look. Let children ask questions or share during the show. Explain that the class needs to send a thank-you letter and pictures, since the officers took time to have their pictures taken. Find out what the children want to say in the letter, and write it for them. See if they have any questions they want to ask the police officers. Leave the letter out for them to illustrate, and then mail it.

Materials

camera, slide film, slide projector and screen, large sheet of craft paper, various art supplies

Other Ideas

- Arrange for the children to deliver the thank-you letter.

- Select other safety helpers to highlight in a slide show.

- Show many different types of safety helpers in the slide show and let children identify each type of helper.

- Let children make a mobile of police-related pictures.

Ambulance on the Run

See if children have had any experiences with paramedics or ambulances. Let them tell their stories. Show them the calendar and explain when the paramedics will visit. Ask the paramedics to share with the children what they do, show any of the tools they use, and let the children tour the ambulance. Take pictures of the visit to show children, and ask what they remember. Share the pictures with the children's families. Send some of the pictures and a story to the local news media.

Materials

camera and film, calendar

Other Ideas

- Invite a family member to tell any family stories about experiences with ambulances.
- Invite children to build an ambulance from a large cardboard box.
- Read *Madeline*, by Ludwig Bemelmans (New York: Viking, 1963).

We've Got Your Number

Draw a large "911" with chalk on a sidewalk or tricycle path. Explain that this is the number a lot of people call on the telephone if they need help from firefighters, police officers, or an ambulance. Tell them they can practice on the play phones in the classroom later. Encourage children to interact with the 911 you have written on the sidewalk in these and other ways: walk on it, jump over it, tiptoe on it, walk backwards on it, push a car on it, roll a ball on it, dance on it, trace over it with more chalk, sing to it, tell it a story, and tell it good-bye and go inside. Let children select any material in the room (blocks, beads, scarves, lids, playdough, paint, yarn) and make a 911. Urge each person to do something different. Take a picture of each 911 creation to make a "911 Book." Follow-up in learning centers to reinforce 911 and how to make the call.

Materials

classroom supplies for making the 911 creations, variety of telephones, camera and film, glue, paper, tape, chalk, pavement or large cardboard surface

Other Ideas

- Visit a place that sells telephones, including cellular phones, to see the variety.
- Invite a 911 operator to talk with children and answer their questions.
- Role-play calling for help.
- List questions about 911 and mail them to the 911 service.
- Invite someone who has called 911 before to share that experience with the children.

Chapter 8

For My Good Health

As young children develop, they begin to make more and more choices that affect their health and well-being. Since much of their early behavior is monitored by adults, children often are unsure or unaware of the choices they have. Sometimes, when they have no model for how to make choices themselves or lack understanding of the consequences of the choices they make, children may inadvertently make unhealthy or unwise decisions.

The purpose of this theme is to help children begin to identify what they can do to help maintain their health and well-being. The activities and materials presented will allow children to practice making decisions and exhibiting behaviors that promote good health.

Addressing Diversity

Family beliefs and attitudes regarding health, illness, drug use, and treatment vary. Some families elect to use no medical support, and others may use healthcare that is unfamiliar. In some families, drugs may be regarded as dangerous, and others may see them as recreational or necessary for treatment of health problems.

Access to money and the values related to it also influence decisions about healthcare and health products. Each family's definition of need will be based on their purchasing ability and the values and experiences they have. These same things will influence the messages given to children and the choices they will be allowed to make. Recognize that each family has the right to make their own health decisions.

Where Will the Theme Lead?

Use these words to stimulate ideas for follow-up activities:

dosage	mail order	counselor	pills	credit
disinfect	discount	meditation	rehabilitation	receipt
injection	measles	vitamins	commercial	yellow pages
dependence	virus	advertisement	generic	consignment
billboard	physical	liquor	currency	lay away

Learning Center Materials

Dramatic Play:
price tags on clothes
billfolds and purses
cash register
syringe without needle
empty medicine containers
adhesive bandages
first-aid tape
ice pack
shopping cart or basket

Table Toys:
coupons to match
coins to sort
price tags to match
coupons cut into puzzles
health containers and lids to match
tweezers and cotton balls
medicine bottles and lids to match outlines
miniature blocks and props for hospital

Language Arts:
ledger and receipts
catalogs
medicine advertisements
cigarette, alcohol, and
  health supply ads
pretend blank checks
pretend bills
pretend credit cards
prescription pad
"no smoking" signs

Science:
packing material samples
coins and tracing paper for rubbings
ink pads and stamps
water and syringe without needle
eyedropper and colored water
microscope
cotton swabs and spices
cash register
medicine resource book
ice to observe

Blocks:
health product boxes
packing materials
play coins for hauling
delivery vehicles
store signs
shopping bags
cotton swabs for building and hauling
medicine bottles and lids
empty health product containers
newspaper ads

Art:
coupons for gluing or cutting
ledger paper
health product containers
cash register paper rolls
newspaper strips
packing materials
syringe without needle for painting
eyedroppers for painting
tissue paper
cotton and toilet paper tubes

Outdoors:
packing materials to glue to wood
medicine boxes for nailing to wood
cardboard pieces to make billboards
large boxes to make store signs
water with basters, eyedroppers,
  and syringe without needle
plastic gloves
delivery signs for child vehicles
herb garden
garden tools

Library Books:
Abuela's Weave, by Omar S.
  Castaneda (New York: Lee
  and Low, 1993).
The Velveteen Rabbit, by Margery Williams
  (New York: Holt, 1983).
You Can Call Me Willy, by Joan C. Verniero
  (New York: Magination, 1995).

Topic 1
Preventing Disease

Learning Objectives:

☑ Children will state how germs can be spread.

☑ Children will cover mouth/nose when coughing or sneezing.

Young children are exposed to germs in many ways. They put items in their mouths, they explore through touching, they put their fingers into their mouths, and they are close to ground and floor level where there are a multitude of germs. Besides being exposed to more germs, young children's bodies do not have as much resistance to illness because their immune system is still developing. Some diseases, such as measles and mumps, are only preventable through immunization, and children do not complete the full series of vaccinations until about age six.

Staff can help prevent the spread of disease through the use of established procedures. Clearly state the policies on immunizations and handling illness so that staff and parents or guardians know how to proceed to better ensure the health of enrolled children, their families, and their caregivers.

All children and adults should have up-to-date immunizations, with the only exceptions based on documented medical or religious reasons. It is recommended that policies address attendance of children and staff with communicable diseases, and dealing with children who become sick while in the classroom.

Disease prevention focuses on preventing the spread of all communicable diseases, regardless of whether a child or adult has a cold, diarrhea, head lice, or HIV/AIDS. Disease prevention includes hand washing and taking precautions to avoid contact with blood or body fluids, including mucous, saliva, urine, feces, or vomit. Staff should wear disposable gloves and wash their hands after removing and disposing the gloves.

Teach children to avoid touching blood or body fluids and help them understand that germs can be carried through these fluids. Children are better able to understand these procedures as related to diseases with which they are familiar, such as colds.

Creating the Environment

Use pictures, books, puzzles, and conversations that include people of different gender, race, and cultures as healthcare professionals. Also include some nontraditional healthcare techniques, such as home remedies, massage, or hydrotherapy. Incorporate both name brand and generic healthcare products in the classroom centers and activities. An environment that includes easy access to a sink with warm running water, soap, paper towels, tissues, and a trash can is recommended. Learning centers may include disposable gloves, spray bottles filled with clean water, clean sponges, and other items used in cleaning.

Areas such as sand and water tables or changing tables should be cleaned and disinfected after each use. Cots may be cleaned and disinfected weekly. A bleach and water solution of 1/4 cup bleach to 1 gallon water, or 1 tablespoon bleach to 1 quart water, is an effective and inexpensive general disinfectant. Areas soiled with blood or body fluids can be disinfected with a solution of 1/4 cup bleach to 1 quart water. Solutions must be made daily since effectiveness lasts only 12 hours. Keep bleach and unused solution in a locked cabinet or closet.

Evaluation:

☒ During role-playing, are children talking about how to avoid germs?

☒ Are children covering their mouths and noses when coughing or sneezing?

☒ Do children role-play or talk about taking or giving immunizations?

Family Information & Activity

Bulletin

Preventing Disease

Runny noses, sniffles, or colds can be caused by bacteria, viruses, allergies, or breathing smoke. Respiratory diseases, such as colds and flu, are spread by eating or drinking from a sick person's utensils, playing with their toys, or just being near someone who has a cold or flu. Cold weather does not cause colds. Though antibiotics and other medicines cannot cure your child of a cold caused by a virus, cold medicines, acetaminophen (such as Tylenol), or cough syrup may help your child feel better. A cool-mist humidifier may ease breathing.

Sometimes harmful bacteria cause a sinus or ear infection. If your child has yellow or green runny mucus, ear pain, or a fever, call your doctor. Do not take your child to school or child care if fever is present. Fever is a sign of contagious disease.

Family Activity

☒ Look at magazines with your child and talk about any pictures where people are doing things to stay healthy and prevent disease. Examples include hand washing, eating healthy foods, exercising, covering sneezes and coughs, taking vitamins, or getting immunizations.

Ideas Please

☒ Give us ideas of who to visit to learn about how germs are spread and how to avoid them.

☒ Please let us know about any serious illness your child has had or experiences with sick people that may make this topic sad or frightening.

Items Please

☒ We will be using cotton balls, cotton swabs, and toilet paper rolls for play.

☒ We need magazine pictures of people who look like they are sick or in pain.

Children's Activities

Invisible

Invite a magician to perform for children. Help children learn about "invisible" and "out of sight" by watching things disappear during the show. Tell children that germs also are invisible, and that they will get to learn more about germs later. Invite a local television station to visit and report on the magic show and study of germs.

Materials
provided by magician

Other Ideas

- Perform a few magic tricks yourself and teach them to the children.
- Play hide-and-seek with objects and talk about how the objects are still there even if the children can't see them.
- Play a game of hide-and-seek with children and discuss how they don't really disappear but are out of sight when hiding.

Secret Spray

Let children spray lemon juice on a sheet of paper and see that it barely shows up. The paper can then be ironed or put into an oven for about ten minutes. At this point, the spray will become visible. Tell children that when they cough or sneeze, they spray invisible germs, just like the spray on the paper.

Safety Note: Use caution when operating an iron or oven with children near. Be sure adequate supervision is available, and never leave the appliance unattended.

Materials
lemon juice, spray bottles, paper, iron or oven

Other Ideas

- Ask children to describe times they sneezed or coughed.
- Let children tell about a time they were sick and how they felt.
- Mix paint in spray bottles and let children spray designs on cardboard boxes.
- Let children use spray bottles filled with water outside.

Invisible Germs

Since germs are not visible to the naked eye, most young children will develop minimal understanding about them, but the concept can still be introduced. Care should be taken not to frighten children about germs. Read *Those Mean Nasty Dirty Downright Disgusting but…Invisible Germs* (*Esos Desagradables Detestables Sucios Completamente Asquerosos pero…Invisibles Gérmenes*), by Judith Rice. Encourage children to talk about the book and ask questions. Point out that everyone who is sick is not contagious, and some diseases are not transmittable. Keep a list of the questions so you can help them find the answers. Tell them that you will look for resource books and experts to help with their questions.

Illustration from *Those Mean Nasty Dirty Downright Disgusting but…Invisible Germs.*

Materials

paper, marker, *Those Mean Nasty Dirty Downright Disgusting but…Invisible Germs*, by Judith Rice (St. Paul: Redleaf, 1997)

Other Ideas

- Let children talk about people they know who are sick.

- Remind children that some people who are sick are not contagious.

- Invite someone who has a disease that is not contagious to visit and tell about the disease.

Germ Experts

Arrange to visit a high school, college, or other community science lab to learn about germs. Request that children be allowed to look at germs through a microscope and have an opportunity to ask questions. Perhaps a science teacher can be available or can arrange for a class to help children look for germs and answer their questions. Prepare the children for the visit in advance. Make a list of questions the children want to ask about germs during their visit. Help children prepare a thank-you poster to send to the lab after they visit.

Materials

list of questions, supplies provided by lab, art supplies

Other Ideas

- Visit a hospital lab to learn about germs.

- Invite a doctor, nurse, or scientist to visit the classroom and tell about germs.

Germ Review

Ask children to tell you what they know about germs. Listen to what they know and the questions they still have. Talk about magic tricks and how, even though you cannot see something, it does not mean it is really gone. Ask them to recall what they learned about germs in the lemon juice activity ("Secret Spray") and the microscope activity ("Germ Experts"). Ask if they have comments. Remind them that germs are everywhere and some of them can cause us to get sick. Reassure the children that they can do some things to help keep healthy, and see how many ways of doing this they can name. Use props to encourage children to talk about eating healthy foods, washing their hands, and not sharing drinking cups, straws, spoons, forks, chopsticks, or anything that goes into the mouth. Remind children to use a tissue to cover coughs and sneezes, and to turn away from someone else when they cough or sneeze. Introduce immunizations by explaining that we also help ourselves stay healthy by seeing a doctor and taking some medicine that keeps us from getting sick.

Materials

tissue, soap, paper towel, drinking cup, spoon, straw, fork, chopsticks, medicine bottle, syringe, healthy foods (such as apples, bread, carrots)

Other Ideas

- Encourage children to write a song about germs. Tape record songs and send the tape to local radio stations.
- Let children create a class mural with pictures of germs.

Topic 2

When I Take Medicine

Learning Objectives:

☑ Children will identify individuals who can give them medicine.

☑ Children will state that it is appropriate to take medicine when sick and to prevent disease.

☑ Children will identify pills as medicine to be taken only when given by an appropriate individual.

It is essential that teachers gather as much information as possible from families regarding their beliefs about the use of medicine and procedures for administering it. In this way, children can receive information and support appropriate to their individual situations.

Although some children are exposed to drug misuse and abuse in their homes or communities, it is not appropriate to present information on illegal drug use or drug abuse to young children. Instead, present information about when to take medicine and from whom to accept medicine.

Program policy on administration of medicine to children should be clear and include who can give the medicine at school, what paperwork is required prior to administration of medicine, where medicine should be stored, and what documentation is necessary. Ask about possible side effects and be prepared to deal with those noted.

Creating the Environment

Keep medicine to be administered in locked containers and store as directed. Provide many types of clean and empty medicine containers for children to see as they learn about taking or applying medicines. Examples of containers to include are pill boxes and bottles, cream and lotion boxes and bottles, spray bottles, and syringes without needles.

During role-playing children can use paper to write prescriptions, make medicine labels, or write instructions for taking medicine. Include resource books, magazines, or computer programs that show pictures of pills and other medicines.

Evaluation:

☒ Are children discussing who can give them medicine?

☒ During role-playing, are children identifying appropriate times to take medicine?

☒ Can children identify pills as medicine?

Family Information & Activity

Bulletin

When I Take Medicine

When your child needs medicine, it is helpful to ask the doctor questions such as: "What is the name of the medicine?" "Does it need to be kept in the refrigerator?" "How much should I give in each dose?" "When and for how long should I give it?" "Should I give the medicine at mealtime?" "Are there any side effects to watch for or be concerned about?" "How long before the medicine starts to work and how will I know if it is?"

Find out more about immunizations for your child by asking your doctor or by contacting the American Academy of Pediatrics (see the "Resources" section).

Family Activities

☒ Let your child use an eyedropper or baster to play in water. Explain that people can take medicine many different ways (drops, pills, cream, shots, liquids).

☒ Explain to your child who can give medicine to them and what they should do if someone else tries to give them medicine.

Ideas Please

☒ Give us ideas of who to visit to help children learn about medicine and when to take it.

☒ Please let us know about any experiences with medicine or family beliefs that will help us individualize this topic for your child.

Items Please

☒ We will be using many empty medicine boxes, bottles, and lids for play.

☒ We need magazine pictures of medicine and people taking medicine and practicing other positive health treatment.

Children's Activities

Pills and Potions

Show children pictures of common over-the-counter medicine for children and ask if they know what it is. Encourage them to tell about experiences they have had with medicine. Ask what they know about medicine and what they would like to know. Write what they say on a large sheet of paper and use it for planning and reviewing. Mention that children should not take medicine unless it is given by an adult that their parents or guardians tell them is okay.

Materials

newsprint, marker, mounted pictures of children's vitamins and cold medicine

Other Ideas

- Visit a store to see many different medicine cabinets.
- Help children make puzzles from pictures of medicine.
- Assist children in making a book that includes pictures of different medicines.
- Let children create individual displays by gluing clean and empty medicine containers inside empty shoeboxes.

A Close Look

Display a variety of medicine containers, pictures of medicine, vitamins glued and laminated to cards, and different medical tools. Invite children to examine the display and talk about what they see. Help them to identify the different ways medicine can look (liquid, pills) and can be taken (shots, drops, chewing, swallowing, drinking). Show them a container with a prescription and explain how some medicine can be purchased by adults at any time, while other medicine can only be purchased if a doctor says so. Remind them that they should only take medicine if their parents or guardians tell them it is all right to do so.

Safety Note: Be sure containers are empty and cleaned. Do not leave pills used for display unattended, and after the activity, remove them. Even dietary supplements like iron tablets can be extremely toxic for young children.

Materials

syringes without needles, medicine container with eyedropper, cream medicine container, spray-on medicine container, vitamins glued to cards and laminated, liquid medicine container, medicine spoon, medicine cup, prescription and over-the-counter bottles

Other Ideas

- Visit a pharmacy to learn about different kinds of medicine.
- Invite a pharmacist to visit and tell about his/her job.
- Invite a veterinarian to display and tell about medicine for animals.
- Help children attach medicine boxes, plastic bottles, and pictures to a 1 by 6 inch piece of untreated pine several feet long.

Now and Then

Show children several different containers of children's vitamins and ask if they know what kind of medicine it is and when to take it. Talk with children about how sometimes we take medicine to help us stay healthy (vitamins and immunizations) and sometimes we take medicine to help us get well. Let the children talk about their experiences with taking medicine.

Materials

children's vitamin containers

Other Ideas

- Invite a doctor to talk about when to take medicine.
- Invite family members to tell about the medicine they take and why.
- Read *Mommies Don't Get Sick,* by Marylin Hafner (Cambridge, MA: Candlewick, 1995).

Botany

Introduce the word *botany* and explain that it is the study of plants. Ask if children have ideas about why people would study plants. Possible reasons would be that some plants are used in medicine, and some plants are used for food, fuel, building supplies, and clothing. Show them an aloe vera plant and explain how it can be used to soothe burns. Let them gently feel the plant inside and out. Tell children that although some plants are used for food and medicine, it is really hard to tell which ones are used for which purpose. Explain that some plants are poisonous. Children should never taste a plant or its seeds or berries unless they ask an adult first, and they should always wash their hands after touching plants. Invite children to go outside and examine some plants and look in a plant guidebook to identify them.

Safety Note: Warn children about aloe vera thorns, and tell them not to taste the plant. Supervise to ensure that hands are washed after the activity, and remove the plant.

Materials

plastic gloves, magnifying glasses, field guide

Other Ideas

- Visit a nature preserve and take a guided tour.
- Visit an herb garden and learn how herbs are used for medicine.
- Gather leaves to press between wax paper or blotting paper, in books, or between bricks.

The Natural Way

Show children a display of natural remedies and ask what they can tell you about them. Explain that some people use natural remedies, like heat, ice, and certain foods, instead of medicine. Some people use honey for sore throats, bee stings, or for dry skin. Tell them soda may be used to ease itching. Let them mix soda and water for a baby doll bath. Remind them that they should let an adult know if they hurt or think they need medicine.

Materials

several kinds of ice packs, ice, several kinds of heating pads, hot water bottle, humidifier, honey, soda, doll, doll bathtub, water

Other Ideas

- Visit a natural health store to see remedies.
- Invite parents to tell about the natural remedies they use.
- Invite a doctor to tell about alternatives to prescribed medicine.
- Help children identify different ways to apply ice instead of using a commercial ice pack.

Topic 3
Drug Use Prevention

Learning Objectives:

☑ Children will state ways tobacco may be used.

☑ Children will state how tobacco can affect their bodies.

☑ Children will identify ways alcohol may be used.

☑ Children will state how alcohol can affect their bodies

The intent of this topic is to help children gain an awareness of tobacco and alcohol that will provide a foundation for future decision-making. To begin, teachers may want to show a tobacco plant and tell how it is grown. They can then explain how the plant is used to make cigarettes, cigars, snuff, and chewing tobacco. When discussing the impact of tobacco and alcohol on the body, remember that children most relate to and understand what they can see and experience around them. For example, allowing children to hold a tobacco leaf or particles of tobacco from a cigarette helps them see that the tobacco doesn't produce negative effects through touch. Use questions to encourage discussion and allow children to share their experiences with people who use tobacco around them. Questions might include, "How did it smell?" "How did it look?" "Was there smoke?" "How did the smoke make you feel?" and "Was anything left when the person finished the cigarette or pipe?"

Though children may have difficulty understanding how tobacco can cause harm to the lungs or heart since they cannot see the heart or lungs, these effects can be discussed and followed with activities that help children understand more clearly.

When introducing the topic of alcohol, teachers may want to first explain that it is a liquid found in many products and then begin to identify the products that contain it. Examples are drinks such as beer, wine, liquor, mouthwashes, medicines, cleansers, and various fuel products. Help children understand that alcohol can be helpful in mouthwashes, medicines, skin cleansers, and as engine fuel, but that too much alcohol inside the body can be harmful. Introduce the process that takes place when someone drinks alcohol, and help children understand that drinking even small amounts of alcohol is very dangerous for young children.

Remember, children cannot control adult behavior or their home environment. Since alcohol and tobacco may be commonly used in families, show care and understanding when dealing with these topics. As children become more aware of the impact various chemicals and products have on their bodies, they may become frightened for themselves or family members. Never use statements such as "smoking is bad" or "drinking is not smart." These statements criticize many parents, adults, and family members, and often confuse children.

Creating the Environment

A smoke-free facility reduces the impact of second-hand smoke on children. Keep classrooms, offices, hallways, playgrounds, and vehicles free of smoke, since these areas may all be connected to or used as children's areas. If a smoking area is provided for staff, it should be outdoors in an area where adults are completely out of children's view and where smoke cannot drift into children's areas. Check local and funding regulations regarding smoke-free environments.

Keep playground and entrances clear of debris, including alcohol or tobacco products and containers. Store any product containing alcohol in a locked cabinet.

Evaluation:

☒ Are children discussing the effects of tobacco and alcohol?

☒ In guided activities, are children able to distinguish containers used for tobacco and alcohol?

☒ In role-playing, do children reflect an understanding of the ways that tobacco and alcohol are used?

Family Information & Activity Bulletin

Drug Use Prevention

Alcohol in beer, wine, cough syrup, mouthwash, and other substances can be very dangerous for young children. Alcohol lowers the body's blood sugar, and even a few sips can cause illness, coma, or death for a young child.

Vitamins, tranquilizers, blood pressure pills, and other medicines can poison children. Iron pills cause more fatal drug poisonings than any other medicine. Keep medicines in child-resistant containers stored in a locked cabinet out of children's reach. Many people, including baby sitters, may keep aspirin or other medicine in purses or containers accessible to children. Calling medicine "candy" or saying that it tastes like candy may encourage drug abuse. Make sure your child knows who is allowed to administer medicine, such as teachers and doctors.

Family Activities

☒ Watch public service advertisements or public service videos with your child that are about cigarette smoking and alcohol use and talk about what they mean.

☒ Your child should know how to respond to invitations to smoke a cigarette, chew tobacco, or drink alcohol. Explain to your child the appropriate responses to such invitations.

Ideas Please

☒ Let us know if you have an idea about a field trip, someone to invite as a guest speaker, or other sources of information for teaching your child about drug use prevention.

Items Please

☒ We will be using drug, alcohol, and tobacco advertisements, signs, and empty containers.

Children's Activities

Labels and Ads

Ask children to collect tobacco and alcohol ads from magazines and newspapers. Encourage them to talk about what they collected. Show them clean and empty alcohol and tobacco containers, pointing out the many different kinds. Read aloud to children the labels from the ads and containers. Tell children about the various ways people use tobacco, as in cigarettes, cigars, pipes, snuff, and chewing tobacco. Talk with children about the ways alcohol is sometimes used in food preparation, medicine, drinks, and fuels. Read and explain the warnings from the ads.

Materials

alcohol containers, tobacco and alcohol advertisements, mouthwash container, cough syrup bottle, tobacco product cartons and containers, pipe

Other Ideas

- Help children make puzzles by gluing tobacco and alcohol ads to cardboard and cutting them into puzzles pieces.

- Match ads to containers.

- Visit a tobacco patch to see the plant at different stages of growth.

- Visit a refinery or brewery to see the ingredients and the process.

- Display a "no smoking" sign and ask children where they might see one.

Television Time

Watch a public service announcement or public service video regarding drug use prevention and discuss the advertisement or video during group time.

Materials

television and VCR, public service video on drug use prevention

Other Ideas

- View with children a videotape of a healthcare professional speaking on drug use prevention.

- Help children create a videotape of their collection of tobacco and alcohol ads and labels.
- Play "Jimmy Says," by Pat Benatar (*Free To Be…A Family.* A&M, 5196).

Health Professional Visit

Visit a health clinic, health department, or doctor's office to have a healthcare professional explain what happens to the smoke when someone smokes a cigarette and what happens to the alcohol when someone drinks liquor. Ask the health professional to explain or describe the effects the alcohol and smoke have on the body, using charts, props, or displays.

Materials
materials determined by health professional

Other Ideas

- Invite a health professional to visit the classroom to explain about smoke and alcohol and their effects on the body.

Don't Start—The Easiest Way to Quit

Invite someone who is trying to stop smoking or drinking to the classroom to tell why they want to stop, to explain what they are doing to stop, and to describe how their body feels while they are trying to quit.

Materials
none needed

Other Ideas

- Invite an adult who lives with a smoker or excessive drinker to tell about their feelings.
- Invite someone who has stopped smoking or drinking to share their experience.
- Look at and discuss nicotine patches or other nicotine substitutes.

What I Know Video

Have children form groups to practice telling one another what they know or have learned about alcohol and tobacco. After children have practiced telling what they know, ask the groups to tell what they know to the large group, and make a videotape of the presentations. If the video does not include private family information, use it in parent training or send it to a local television or radio stations to use as a public service announcement.

Materials

video camera, television, VCR, props

Other Ideas

- Help children make a "how to stop smoking" video.

- Assist children to make a "what happens to your body when you smoke/drink" video.

- Allow children to use alcohol and tobacco ads and containers in a display about preventing drug use.

Topic 4
How I Get What I Need

Learning Objectives:

☑ Children will identify items that are needed every day (food, clothes, shoes, soap, toothpaste).

☑ Children will begin using vocabulary related to consumerism (buy, sale, credit, shop, purchase).

☑ Children will identify various ways to access health-care and healthcare products.

There are many items people can buy and many ways to obtain products and services. By making the children aware of the variety of choices, teachers can begin to help children identify products and services that are needed and those that are not needed.

When viewing newspaper, magazine, and television advertisements with children, be sure that a wide range of products and services are represented. Introduce children to many places to shop, such as malls, church-sponsored stores, flea markets, street vendors, consignment shops, Goodwill and Salvation Army stores, farmers' markets, yard sales, and pawn shops.

It is also useful to include a variety of methods that might be used to obtain services or products. These include purchase orders, coins, money, gift certificates, credit, cash, check, bartering, trading, food stamps, insurance cards, coupons, and debit cards. As you study the various methods of payment, encourage interest and discussion regarding currency from other countries.

Help children understand that many people make their own products and grow their own food. Others know how to repair broken items and use home health remedies.

Creating the Environment

Allow children to set up a special store, clinic, or restaurant center so they can role-play being a consumer and making choices. Provide a variety of product and service advertisements, price tags, shopping lists, bills, receipts, ledgers, budgets, loan applications, play money, play credit cards, cash registers, phones, credit card machines, and boxes and shopping bags. Paper, poster board, and cardboard is helpful for children to use in making signs, billboards, and advertisements. Introduce currency from other countries and use words from other languages to describe or name products and services.

Evaluation:

☒ Are children talking about different kinds of products and services that are needed?

☒ Are children role-playing and using a variety of words to describe obtaining products and service?

☒ Are children role-playing various methods for accessing products and services?

Family Information & Activity Bulletin

How I Get What I Need

Shopping with your child is a way to model decision-making. When selecting items to purchase, talk about what you are buying and why. This will help children see that adults make choices about what they buy, rather than buying everything on the shelf.

When purchasing over-the-counter medicines, such as pain relievers or cold remedies, you can read the label with your child and discuss what the medicine is for. This helps your child understand that medications have a specific purpose and should only be taken as needed. Children

may help you select health-related products, such as soap, shampoo, or toothpaste. You can discuss how you use them, select the scent or color you prefer, and compare prices on different brands. Promote a feeling of independence by allowing your child to select the product, such as colorful bandages or a particular toothpaste.

Family Activities

- Show your child the health-related products you use. Talk about how your family gets them.
- Let your child help put healthcare products away after shopping.
- View and discuss television, newspaper, and billboard healthcare advertisements with your child.

Ideas Please

- If you wish, tell us where you get healthcare supplies so we can talk about it with your child.

Items Please

- Send the class any empty containers for healthcare products, advertisements about health products, coupons you won't be using, boxes, and paper and plastic bags.

Children's Activities

Shoes, Soap, and Soup

Give children bags and boxes that contain food, clothing, and health-related products. Have each child select one or two items. Let children tell about their selections and why they picked that item. Talk about products they use every day and whether the items are necessary or not. Encourage children to look at their selections to find a price tag or bar code. Briefly discuss cost.

Materials

bags (paper, plastic, and canvas), boxes, clothes, food containers, containers for generic and name brand health-related products (toothpaste, soap, shampoo, vitamins)

Other Ideas

- Visit a store to see products we use daily and find out how much they cost.
- Visit a store and buy health-related products.
- Help children create a bar code scanner for role-playing.

Bag It, Box It

Exhibit a variety of shopping bags and boxes for children to describe and compare. Explain that when you buy something, you usually get a container in which to carry it, although some people bring their own containers as a way to recycle. Let children open boxes that contain different packing materials, talk about what each is, and why it might be used. Encourage children to talk about their experiences in stores, asking them what they saw and about the people who worked there.

Safety Note: To avoid danger of suffocation, plastic bags should not be used.

Materials

bags and boxes (large, medium, small, plastic, paper, canvas, netting, plain, colorful, with handles, without handles, for hang-up clothes, for shoes, for hats, for potatoes), packing materials (shredded and wadded newspaper, Styrofoam peanuts, Styrofoam blocks, foam, bubble wrap)

Other Ideas

- Go for a "bag walk" in a shopping center and request a bag from several stores to display and study.
- Investigate bags made and used by people from many cultures.

- Give each child a paper or plastic bag and let them decorate it creatively.
- Add packing materials to different learning centers for creative use.

Places to Shop

Prepare a slide show of many places to obtain products or services. Consider including a flea market, farmers' market, yard sale, pawn shop, consignment store, discount store, Goodwill and Salvation Army store, street vendor, donation center, mall, public library, health department, military post exchange, and ethnic grocery. After viewing the slide show, let children look at catalogs and explain that some people order items and receive them in the mail instead of going to a store. Tell them people place orders by telephone, mail, fax, and computer.

Materials
camera and slide film, slide projector, screen, product catalogues

Other Ideas
- Visit a variety of places to shop with children and take pictures.
- Invite families to visit and tell about places they shop.
- Allow children to help choose a book or tape to order for classroom use and then help them complete the order form.
- Read *Fruit and Vegetable Man,* by Roni Schotter (Boston: Joy Street, 1993).
- Play "Down on Grandpa's Farm," by Raffi (*One Light One Sun.* Shoreline, 10040).

Ways to Pay

Display coin banks and give each child some coins to put in them. Let children tell you what they know about money. Ask what people do with money. See if they know of ways to purchase items other than using money. Fill a wooden bowl with the various methods of payment (see materials list below). Tell the children that inside are things some people use to buy products and services. Let children examine the items and talk about them. Explain that you are going to use them for a bulletin board exhibit. They can help you with the exhibit.

Materials
coin banks, wooden bowl, methods of payment (gift certificates, coupons, tokens, food stamps, barter agreements, simulated credit card, pretend checks, coins, dollar

bills, foreign currency, billing statement, simulated insurance card, simulated medical card, library card, simulated gas card)

Other Ideas

- Visit a bank and explore the machines and what people that work there do.
- Invite people to show and tell about money from other countries.
- Learn about how money is made and make some for role-playing.
- Visit a place that sells cash registers and explore the different ones.
- Play "Magic Penny," by Tickle Tune Typhoon (*Circle Around*. Tickle Tune Typhoon Records).

Create, Repair, and Reuse

Show children homemade materials and items in need of repair and talk about how sometimes things can be homemade or fixed instead of purchased. Invite discussion about children's experiences with cleaning, repairing, or making things.

Materials

shoes in need of repair, dirty or torn garments, clothing pattern, handmade toys, carpentry tools

Other Ideas

- Visit a shoe repair shop.
- Visit a seamstress, tailor, or alteration shop.
- Invite a family member to make or repair something while children watch.
- Taste food from a family garden.
- Read *The Big Green Pocketbook*, by Candice Ransom and Felicia Bond (New York: Harper, 1993).

Resources

National Agencies and Organizations

American Academy of Pediatrics
PO Box 927, Elk Grove Village, IL 60009
Phone: 800-433-9016
Internet: http://www.aap.org/.
Source of staff and parent information related to child health and safety.

American Association of Poison Control
Internet: http://198.79.220.3/aapcc.htm.
Directory of centers, educational materials, resource guides, technology issues, software information, and news.

American Public Health Association
1015 15th Street NW, Washington, DC 20005
Source of health-related materials.

American School Health Association
PO Box 708, Kent, OH 44240-0708
Phone: 800-445-2742
Internet: http://www.mgi-net.com/mgilists/asha.htm.
Available resources include *Journal of School Health, Hip on Health*, and other low-cost publications related to school health.

American Society for Testing & Materials (ASTM)
100 Barr Harbor Drive, West Conshohocken, PA 19428-2959
Phone: 610-832-9585, Fax: 610-832-9555
Internet: http://www.astm.org.
Source for detailed information on playground site and surface testing standards, including the *Safety Performance Specification for Playground Equipment for Public Use.*

Association for the Advancement of Health Education
1900 Association Drive, Reston, VA 22091
Phone: 800-213-7193
Internet: http://www.aahpred.org.
Resources provided include *Journal of Health Education, Health Education Teaching Ideas*, and other low-cost publications related to school and community health.

Association for Childhood Education International (ACEI)
11501 Georgia Avenue, Suite 315, Wheaton, MD 20902
Phone: 800-423-3563
Internet: http://www.udel.edu/bateman/acei.
A playground safety checklist is available from this source.

Centers for Disease Control and Prevention (CDC)
Internet: http://www.cdc.gov/.
CDC includes eleven centers, institutes, and offices with different information and specialties.

Center for Safety in the Arts
5 Beekman Street, New York, NY 10038
Phone: 212-227-6220, Fax: 212-233-3846
Provides over 100 publications, a quarterly newsletter, telephone technical assistance, and workshops.

Child Safety Forum
Internet: http://www.xmission.com:80/~gastown/safe/safe2.htm.
This site provides safety checklists, handbooks, a parent's bulletin area, and links to other resources on the Internet.

Consumer Information Guide
Pueblo, CO 81009
Phone: 719-948-4000
Internet: http://www.pueblo.gsa.gov/.
Contains description and order information for many free and inexpensive U.S. Government publications that address the health of children and adults.

KidsHealth
The Nemours Foundation, DuPont Hospital for Children
1600 Rockland Road, Wilmington, DE 19803
Internet: http://KidsHealth.org/index2.html/.
This web site is devoted to the health of children and teens. Contains information about growth, food, fitness, childhood infections, and immunizations. Includes *How The Body Works* animations.

National Association for the Education of Young Children
1509 16th Street NW, Washington, DC 20036-1426
Phone: 800-424-2460
Internet: http://www.naeyc.org/naeyc.
Journals, conferences, position statements, books, brochures, videos, and posters are available at low cost.

National Center for Education in Maternal and Child Health
2000 15th Street N, Suite 701, Arlington, VA 22201-2617
Phone: 703-524-7802
Internet: http://www.ncemch.georgetown.edu/NCEMCH.htm.
Extensive publications catalog is available, which includes reports, brochures, fact sheets, curricula, and posters.

National Institutes of Health
Internet: http://www.nih.gov.
Information and toll-free numbers for many health-related resource centers and clearinghouses.

National Program for Playground Safety
University of Northern Iowa, School for Health, Physical Education, and Leisure Services
Cedar Falls, Iowa 50614-0161
Phone: 800-554-PLAY, Fax: 319-273-5833
Internet: http://iscssun.uni.edu/coe/playgrnd/main.html.
Provides materials and training on playground development, supervision, and maintenance.

National Resource Center for Health and Safety in Child Care
University of Colorado Health Sciences Center School of Nursing
4200 E Ninth Avenue
Campus Box C287, Denver, CO 80262
Phone: 800-598-KIDS
Internet: http://nrc.uchsc.edu.
Center develops and distributes training and technical assistance and maintains a database of standards, consultants, conferences, and related organizations.

National Safe Kids Campaign
111 Michigan Avenue NW, Washington, DC 20010-2970
Phone: 202-662-0600
Internet: http://www.oclc.org/safekids/.
Safety materials are provided with state and local coalitions implementing community-based strategies to prevent childhood injury.

U.S. Consumer Product Safety Commission (CPSC)
5401 Westbard Avenue, Bethesda, MD 20207
Phone: 800-638-2772
Internet: http://www.cpsc.gov/.
Playground safety tips and handbooks are available.

Information and Materials

Activity Books (Grades K-2)
ETR Network Publications, PO Box 1830, Santa Cruz, CA 95061-1830 (800-321-4407)
Baby Basics (1993), by Elizabeth Raptis Picco
Caring, Sharing, and Getting Along (1993), by Mary Dell Johnson
Germ Smart (1990), by Judith K. Scheer
Masterpiece Me (1993), by Sally Wittman
The Multicultural Caterpillar (1990), by Ana Consuelo Matiella
Our Bodies, Our Cells (1993), by Marilyn Cahn
Safety Is No Accident (1993), by William Kane and Kathleen Herrera
We Are A Family (1990), by Ana Consuelo Matiella
You and Me, Tobacco Free (1990), by Judith K. Scheer

Barney Safety: Parents Guide to Child Safety (1995)
Lyons Group, 2435 N Central Expressway, Suite 1600, Richardson TX 75080 (214-390-6000)

Caring for Our Children...National Health and Safety Performance Standards: Guidelines for Out-of-Home Child Care Programs (1992), American Academy of Pediatrics, PO Box 927, Elk Grove Village, IL 60009 (800-433-9016)

Caring for Our Children...National Health and Safety Performance Standards: Guidelines for Out-of-Home Child Care Programs (1995). Video series. American Academy of Pediatrics, PO Box 927, Elk Grove Village, IL 60009 (800-433-9016)

Child Safety at Home (1992), and *Child Safety Outdoors* (1995). Videos.
KidSafety of America, 4750 Chino Avenue, Suite D, Chino, CA 91710 (800-524-1156)

Childhood Emergencies: What to Do. A Quick Reference Guide (1996), by The Marin Childcare Council. Bull Publishing Company, PO Box 208, Palo Alto, CA 94302-0208 (415-322-2855)

The Corel Child Care CD, by the Corel Medical Series, in association with the Canadian Pediatric Society. TigerSoftware, 8700 W Flagler Street, 4th Floor, Miami, FL 33174-2428 (800-782-1430)

The Crisis Manual for Early Childhood Teachers (1996), by Karen Miller.
Gryphon House, PO Box 207, Beltsville, MD 20704-0207 (800-638-0928)

Critical Issues Series
ETR Network Publications, PO Box 1830, Santa Cruz, CA 95061-1830 (800-321-4407)
    Does AIDS Hurt? (1988), by Marcia Quackenbush, Sylvia Villarreal.
    Handle With Care (1992), by Sylvia Villarreal, Lora-Ellen McKinney, Marcia Quackenbush.
    Am I In Trouble? (1990), by Richard L Curwin, Allen N. Mendler.
    Am I Fat? (1992), by Joanne Ikeda, Priscilla Naworski.
    Are You Sad Too? (1993), by Dinah Seibert, Judy Drolet, Joyce Fetro.
    I Can't Sit Still (1992), by Dorothy Davies Johnson.
    I Don't Feel Good (1991), by Jane Lammers.
    Is It Safe? (1994), by Becky Smith.
    Positively Different (1991), by Ana Consuelo Matiella.
    Smiling at Yourself (1990), by Allen Mendler.
    Tobacco Talk (1991), by Carol D'Onofrio.
    When Sex Is The Subject (1991), by Pamala M. Wilson.

Dusty the Dragon and Dr. Margie Hogan Talk About Tobacco (1990), by Dr. Margie Hogan. Video.
ETR Network Publications, PO Box 1830, Santa Cruz, CA 95061-1830 (800-321-4407)

First Aid for Children—Fast! Emergency Procedures for Parents and Caregivers (1995), by the Johns Hopkins Children's Center. D.K. Publishing, 95 Madison Avenue, New York, NY 10016

The Germ Busters (1996)
KidSafety of America, 4750 Chino Avenue, Suite D, Chino, CA 91710 (800-524-1156)

Health Education Teaching Ideas, Volume II (1995)
American Association for Health Education, 1900 Association Drive, Reston, VA 22091 (800-213-7193)

Health and Safety in Child Care (1991), by Susan S. Aronson.
HarperCollins Publishers, 10 E 53 Street, New York, NY 10022

The Healthy Young Child (1995), by Sari F. Edelstein.
West Publishing, PO Box 64526, 610 Opperman Drive, St. Paul, MN 55164-0526

Healthy Young Children...A Manual for Programs (1991), edited by A.S. Kendrick, R. Kaufmann, and K.P. Messenger. National Association for the Education of Young Children, 1509 16th Street NW, Washington, DC 20036-1426 (800-424-2460)

Here We Go, Watch Me Grow! A Preschool Health Curriculum (1991), by Charlotte Hendricks and Connie Jo Smith. ETR Network Publications, PO Box 1830, Santa Cruz, CA 95061-1830 (800-321-4407)

Hip on Health (1997), parent information and miniposters by Charlotte Hendricks.
American School Health Association, PO Box 708, Kent, OH 44240-0708 (800-445-2742)

Human Race Club Series (1989), by Joy Berry. (Videos for children.)
ETR Network Publications, PO Box 1830, Santa Cruz, CA 95061-1830 (800-321-4407)
   Casey's Revenge: A Story About Fights Between Brothers & Sisters
   The Fair Weather Friend: A Story About Making Friends
   A High Price to Pay: A Story About Earning Money
   The Lean Mean Machine: A Story About Handling Emotions
   The Letter on Light Blue Stationery: A Story About Self-Esteem
   The Unforgettable Pen Pal: A Story About Prejudice & Discrimination

The Learn Not to Burn Preschool Program (1991), National Fire Protection Association, One Batterymarch Park, Quincy, MA 02269-9101 (617-770-0200)

Model Playground Law and Safety Guidelines
Consumers Federation of America, 1424 16th Street NW, Suite 604, Washington, DC 20036 (202-387-6121)

Reaching Potentials: Transforming Early Childhood Curriculum and Assessment, Volume 2 (1995), edited by Sue Bredekamp and Teresa Rosegrant. National Association for the Education of Young Children, 1509 16th Street NW, Washington, DC 20036-1426 (800-424-2460)

Safer Kids! Community Action Guide for Children's Fire Safety Education Program (1994)
BIC Corporation, 500 BIC Drive, Milford, CT 06460

Sooper Puppy Series (Videos for children.)
J. Gary Mitchell Film Company, 1313 Scheibel Lane, Sebastopol, CA 95472 (800-301-4050)
   Drink Drank Drunk (1988)
   Flying High (1988)
   Once Upon a Feeling (1990)
   Puff of Smoke (1988)
   Self-Esteem (1988)
   That's Trouble (1992)
   This, That, or the Other (1991)
   What's the Difference (1990)
   Whose Wuzzit? (1990)
   Words Can Hurt (1989)

Tip Sheets—Parent Information
American Academy of Pediatrics, PO Box 927, Elk Grove, IL 60009 (800-433-9016)

What Tadoo Series (Videos for children.)
J. Gary Mitchell Film Company, 1313 Scheibel Lane, Sebastopol, CA 95472 (800-301-4050)
   Believe Me (1992)
   What Tadoo (1985)
   What Tadoo with Fear (1988)
   What Tadoo with Secrets (1990)

Also From Redleaf Press

All the Colors We Are: The Story of How We Get Our Skin Color – Outstanding full-color photographs showcase the beautiful diversity of human skin color and offers children a simple, accurate explanation of how we are the color we are. Bilingual. English/Spanish on each page.

Busy Fingers, Growing Minds – Go beyond finger plays and songs to include art, creative dramatics and theme expansion. This book is wonderfully complete and is a valuable reference for any early childhood teacher.

The Kindness Curriculum – Over 60 imaginative, exuberant activities that create opportunities for kids to practice kindness, empathy, conflict resolution, respect, and more.

Making It Better: Activities for Children Living in a Stressful World – This important book offers bold new information about the physical and emotional effects of stress, trauma, and violence on children today and gives teachers and caregivers the confidence to help children survive, thrive, and learn.

Open the Door Let's Explore More! – Revised and expanded, this new edition of the popular *Open the Door Let's Explore* is filled with activities to do before, during, and after field trips to reinforce learning while having fun.

Practical Solutions to Practically Every Problem – Over 300 proven developmentally appropriate solutions for all kinds of classroom problems.

Reflecting Children's Lives – A practical guide to help you put children and childhood at the center of your curriculum. Rethink and refresh your ideas about scheduling, observations, play, materials, space, and emergent themes.

So This Is Normal Too? Teachers and Parents Working Out Developmental Issues in Young Children – Makes the challenging behaviors of children a vehicle for cooperation among adults and stepping stones to learning for children.

Star Power for Preschoolers: Learning Life Skills Through Physical Play – An integrated series of sixty physical activities designed to help children develop five specific life success skills: concentration, imagination, relaxation, cooperation, and self-esteem.

Those Icky Sticky Smelly Cavity Causing but...Invisible Germs – An imaginative tool to help children develop good toothbrushing habits. Bilingual. English/Spanish on each page.

Those Mean Nasty Dirty Downright Disgusting but...Invisible Germs – A delightful story that reinforces for children the benefits of frequent hand washing. Bilingual. English/Spanish on each page.

Training Teachers – Original strategies and training tools that bring a new approach to the how of teaching and also support great teacher development.

To order or for more information
on these and other titles call
Redleaf Press
800-423-8309